Cheshire Walks
with Children

Nick Lambert

Published by Sigma Leisure – an imprint of
Sigma Press, 1 South Oak Lane, Wilmslow, Cheshire SK9 6AR, England.

British Library Cataloguing in Publication Data
A CIP record for this book is available from the British Library.

ISBN: 1-85058-560-1

Typesetting and Design by: Sigma Press, Wilmslow, Cheshire.

Cover photograph: Jodrell Bank Radio Telescope *(Nick Lambert)*

Maps and photographs: Nick Lambert

Printed by: MFP Design & Print

Disclaimer: the information in this book is given in good faith and is believed to be correct at the time of publication. No responsibility is accepted by either the author or publisher for errors or omissions, or for any loss or injury howsoever caused. Only you can judge your own fitness, competence and experience.

Preface

Cheshire, with its vast plain and gentle hills, makes ideal walking country for children. I have walked its network of footpaths and quiet bridleways many times with my family, and on numerous occasions have enjoyed spectacular days alone. I hope walking in Cheshire provides you and your family with as much pleasure as it has given me and mine.

All route directions have been checked and double checked, but places change. Houses are sold and sometimes alter their names. Trees are cut down, footpaths are re-routed, a stile can be replaced by a gate and so on. The route maps are only intended as a rough guide to the walk. Please carry the appropriate Ordnance Survey map with you to help you in case you get lost, though hopefully that won't happen.

And finally . . . many of the walks pass meres and rivers where there are many ducks and water birds, so take some bread along; children love feeding ducks, but ducks these days are a health-conscious species and apparently they prefer brown bread, as white bread interferes with their digestive system. So next time you're out shopping, pop a wholemeal loaf in your basket for those fibre-enlightened wildfowl.

Nick Lambert

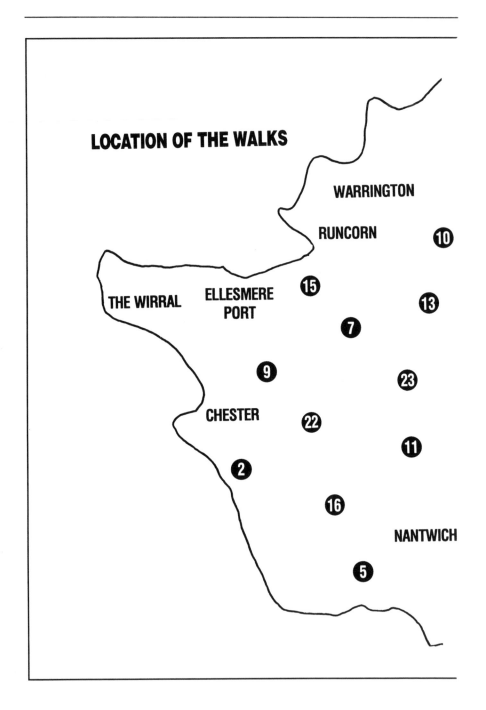

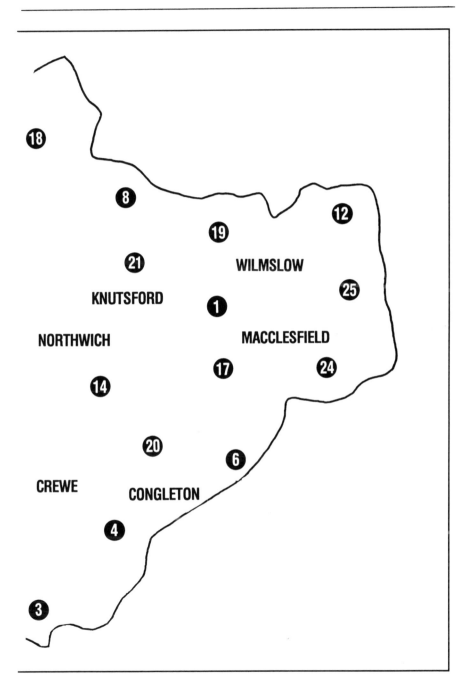

Contents

Before you begin . . .   **1**

Quick Reference Chart   **4**

The Walks

Alderley Edge   **5**

    Distance: *Entire route, 3 miles; Pushchair route about 1 mile*

Aldford   **13**

    Distance: *A gentle 1$^1/_2$ miles (there are no escape routes).*

Audlem   **20**

    Distance: *Entire route: just under 6 miles*
    Shorter route: 3 miles

Barthomley   **29**

    Distance: *Entire route: 3 miles*

Big Mere and Marbury   **36**

    Distance: *Entire route, 6 miles*

The Cloud, Congleton   **43**

    Distance: *Short route: Just under 2 miles*
    Longer route: 4½ miles

Delamere Forest   50
Distance: *6 miles*

Dunham Massey and Little Bollington   57
Distance: *Entire route: 3 miles*

Great Barrow   64
Distance: *4½ miles, with various escape routes.*

Great Budworth and Arley   72
Distance: *6 miles – no escape routes*

Little Budworth   81
Distance: *3 miles*

Lyme Park   87
Distance: *Route A: Entire route, for users of public transport – 6 miles*
Route B: Shorter route for car drivers – 4 miles

Marbury Country Park   95
Distance: *2 miles.*

Over Peover   101
Distance: *Entire route – 6 miles*
Shorter route – 4 miles
Plus various escape routes

Overton Hill   110
Distance: *Entire route: 3 miles*

Peckforton   118
Distance: *Entire route from Beeston – 5½ miles*

Redesmere and Capesthorne   127
Distance: *3 miles*

Risley Moss   134
Distance: *Entire route: a mere mile!*

Styal Woods   139
Distances: *1.5 miles – 3 miles.*

Swettenham   147
Distance: *Entire circular route from Swettenham Arms – 3 miles.*

Tatton Park   155
Distance: *4 miles.*

Wharton's Lock & the Shropshire Union Canal   161
Distance: *Just under 2 miles.*

The Whitegate Way and Vale Royal   166
Distance: *Entire route: 5 miles, with many escape routes.*

Wincle   173
Distance: *Entire route 2 miles.*

Windgather Rocks & Shining Tor   179
Distance: *Entire route 8 miles, with various escape routes.*

50 Questions & Answers for Boring Journeys   189

Ideas for Games on Long Journeys   192

ℬefore you begin . . .

This advice, some of it based on the Country Code, will make walking in the Cheshire countryside even more enjoyable – for you and others.

☆ Don't drop litter. If there is no bin, take it home.

☆ The countryside should be a place of peace and tranquillity. Do not ruin it for other people by shouting and screaming.

☆ Close all gates after you, otherwise animals may stray onto the road and cause an accident. Keep dogs on leads when there are farm animals around, and under close control at all times.

☆ Do not try to get too near to wild animals, as many of them will be frightened and may BITE!

☆ If stroking farm animals such as horses, keep your fingers WELL AWAY from their mouths.

☆ Always stick to the public footpaths/bridleways, and do not stray onto private land.

☆ Some farms use electric fences to separate fields. These are usually a single wire held up by occasional plastic supports. The voltage is low, and won't kill you. Even so, it could give you an unpleasant shock, so don't touch them.

☆ Do not cross railway lines, except by proper crossing places, such as bridges.

☆ Always walk on the right hand side of a lane or road, so that you are walking **towards** the traffic, and can see any approaching vehicle. Keep well into the side of the road and keep in single file. Restrain small children as traffic approaches.

☆ Do not pick wild flowers. Leave them for others to enjoy.

☆ Never eat wild berries. They may look colourful and tasty, but many are deadly poisonous. Mushrooms and toadstools also look attractive, but you should not touch them.

☆ Never fool around near water. Do not paddle in a stream or pond unless an adult says it is safe to do so.

☆ Respect the countryside and enjoy your walk!

A Note about Public Rights of Way

Countryside in any county can change, with the use of fields changing each year. If the footpath across a farmed field is lost under a crop, then you have the right to make your way through that crop and you have the legal right to trespass, where necessary, in order to by-pass any illegal obstacle. Nevertheless, take care not to damage any crop or property.

I'm afraid I encountered many illegally blocked public footpaths, particularly in West Cheshire. As a result I had to amend the walking routes many times to avoid them, so the paths used in the book should all be problem free. All blocked footpaths were duly reported to Cheshire County Council and the Ramblers' Association, and should now have been properly reinstated.

Public Footpaths are in many cases ancient rights of way, and not even the landowner has the right to prevent their use. If you encounter hazards or blocked paths on your walk, then the Ramblers' Association would like to hear from you, but first, always double check the correct route of the right of way on an up-to-date Ordnance Survey map. The main address for the RA is:

> The Ramblers' Association
> 1/5 Wandsworth Road
> London SW8 2XX

Also, there are several local RA groups and you should be able to get details of them from your local library.

Railway Information

Railway information – times, fares etc. – can be obtained from the following British Rail Enquiry Lines:

Manchester: 0161 832 8353

Chester (details from Liverpool Info. line):   0151 709 9696

Crewe: 01782 411411

Bus Information

Information on all bus services within the county can be obtained from Cheshire County Council's Bus Information Line: 01244 602666

Tourist Information Centres

For information on opening times, transport, places to stay and practically anything else, try the Tourist Information Centre. They are usually very helpful and knowledgeable. The telephone numbers of some of the major ones are listed below:

Chester	01244 351609/317962
Knutsford	01565 632611
Macclesfield	01625 504114
Nantwich	01270 610983
Warrington	01925 442180

Introductory Notes on the Text

This is a very unusual book, intended to be read by both parents and children. The following conventions have been used to make the book as useful as possible to both categories:

**Directions are numbered and appear in bold text so that they can be seen at a glance.**

☺ Information for the children is set in a contrasting typestyle. This is to be read aloud, or for them to read themselves. **OTHER INFORMATION FOR PARENTS APPEARS IN BOLD CAPITALS.**

Q/A Questions (and answers) are in the same type style, with "Q" and "A".

In between the instructions you'll often see text that looks like this. We've used this for all sorts of extra information, ranging from background material to escape routes – generally, the sort of thing you can skate over if you're in a rush to complete the main walk.

Checklists appear at the end of each walk, for the children to tick off things as they see them. If you do not want to write in the book, copy the checklist onto a piece of paper, and give one to each child, so they can compete to see who spots the most.

Sketch maps

The maps are intended only as a rough guide to the route and are not drawn to scale. Unless otherwise stated, North is upwards. Not all buildings are shown.

Roads	=	a continuous line
Footpaths	=	a dotted line
P	=	parking
PH	=	public house

Quick Reference Chart

Plan your day at a glance, and check which routes have the features or facilities you require. For more information, see the individual route.

Notes & key

Rail:	routes that are within a short walk of a railway station
Bus:	routes that are within a short walk from a bus stop
Cafe:	cafe or tearoom along the route or within easy walking distance
Pubs:	pub along the route where families are welcome, with seats outside or a family room
Wet weather:	walks suitable for bad weather or winter conditions, usually with gravelled paths or all-weather surfaces
Flat:	route is more or less flat, or can be made flat using escape routes. •• = totally flat circular routes
Historical:	place(s) of historical interest features along the route, or close-by
Pushchairs:	walks with at least a small route suitable for pushchairs, though it may involve some effort •• = complete circular routes that are totally suitable, or can be made suitable, for pushchairs
Features:	places of specific interest to children along the route or close-by

	Rail	Bus	Cafe	Pubs	Wet weather	Flat	Historical	Push chairs	Features
1. Alderley	•	•	•	•			Various	•	Legends, Caves
2. Aldford		•		•		•	Estate Village		
3. Audlem		•	•	•		•		•	Canal & Locks
4. Barthomley		•		•		•	Fighting in Civil War		
5. Big Mere			•						Wildfowl
6. The Cloud							Stone Age Burial		
7. Delamere	•	•	•	•	•	•		••	Visitor Centre. Cycle Hire
8. Dunham Massey		•	•	•		•	Stately Home	••	Deer & Wildlife. Canal
9. Great Barrow	•		•		•				
10. Great Budworth		•		•		•	Estate Village & Hall		
11. Little Budworth		•	•	•				•	Heathland wildlife
12. Lyme Park	•	•	•				Stately Home	•	Deer, ducks, playground
13. Marbury	•	•				•		••	Bird Hide
14. Over Peover			•			•	Stately Home		
15. Overton Hill		•							Views over Mersey estuary
16. Peckforton			•	•			Two castles; estate village	••	Castles, candle workshops
17. Redesmere		•				•	Stately home		Wildfowl
18. Risley Moss	•			•	•			••	Wildlife hides
19. Styal Woods	•	•	•	•	•		Cotton mill; old village	•	Mill/museum
20. Swettenham			•						Nature reserve
21. Tatton Park	•	•	•			•	•	Two halls	••	Deer, bathing, playground
22. Wharton's Lock		•				•	Castle nearby	•	Canal & lock
23. Whitegate Way	•					•	Old railway & station	•	
24. Wincle				•					

𝒜lderley 𝕰dge

Alderley Edge is a popular spot for Sunday walks and days out. In Summer, it can be very busy in the car parks and on the main paths, but there are still areas where you can walk in peace and solitude, such as Waterfall Wood, on the western fringes. Alderley is a mysterious place with tales about witches, wizards, and things that go bump in the night. The Edge and surrounding area provided an eerie setting for Alan Garner's epic tales "The Weirdstone of Brazinghamen" and "The Moon of Gomrath". Garner's family lived for generations in a cottage at the foot of the Edge, and he chronicles their story in "The Stone Book Quartet".

Alderley was once the site of much mining activity. The dangerous mines are now all sealed and the Edge is under the guardianship of the National Trust.

Starting point:	Main car park (SJ860773) off Macclesfield road (B5087) between Macclesfield and Alderley Edge village.
By rail:	Alderley Edge station. Walk through the village to the roundabout and take the Macclesfield road, uphill, to the Edge.
Distance:	Entire route, 3 miles; Pushchair route about 1 mile
Terrain:	Good gravelled paths at the top of the Edge. Winding paths at the bottom, prone to muddiness in wet weather.
Maps:	OS Landranger 118
Public Toilets:	Main car park
Refreshments:	Wizard Tea-room, near to main car park. Open only at weekends. Other places in Alderley village.
Pushchairs:	Short pushchair route. Begin with direction 1.

1. **From the main car park follow the pathway to the Wizard Tea-rooms. (On entering the car park, it is on the left.)**

☺ This was once an old barn which has been made into a tea-room. It is built of rough stone which has been painted white. At the side you can see an old stable door. The top part could be opened so that horses could see outside. Above is a door to the loft, where hay, for the animals to eat in Winter, would have been kept.

(Next to the tea-room is a National Trust information room. Information about the caves and history of the Edge.)

2. **From the tea-room, continue along the driveway towards the woods. Bear left before the warden's house, following the path between the trees. (Marked as being suitable for wheelchairs.)**

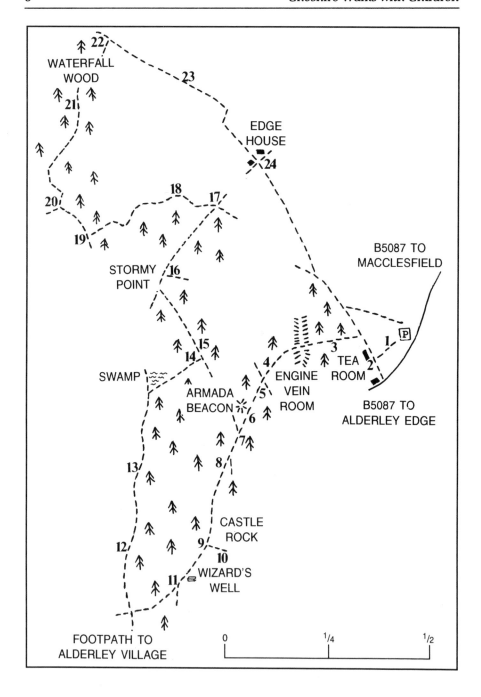

3. **Keep to the main path straight ahead.**

☺ Over 250 years ago there were no trees at Alderley Edge; it was bare rock, heather and low bushes. Lord Stanley, who owned much of the land around Alderley, planted Scots Pines, and later birch, on the highest points of the Edge. It was then fenced off and became private. On certain days the local villagers were allowed to visit the woods.

4. **Cut straight across the sandy area and continue into the woods, still signed for wheelchairs.**

☺ (**AT THE SANDY AREA: INDICATE THE ROCKY FAULT LINE TO THE RIGHT WHICH IS ENGINE VEIN MINE.**) This is a mine which at one time was worked for copper. It is thought that mining may have taken place at Alderley as early as Roman times, certainly it has gone on for several hundred years. There is no mining here now.

There are no natural caves at Alderley. All the tunnels in the earth are man-made mines. People who explore caves and mines are called *pot-holers*. You may see some around the Edge, probably wearing safety helmets with lights on the front, so they can see in the darkness underground. If they have just come out of one of the mines, they will probably be covered with sandy-coloured mud! There are entrances into the mines on either side of the path, but they are now blocked by manhole covers.

(The larger mines are sealed and closed to the public, as they have been the cause of accidents and several deaths over the years. Supervised trips can be arranged, usually for Sunday afternoons. The pot-holers have a lock-up just around the corner from the National Trust information room. Ask there for details.)

5. **Continue into the woods, still signed for wheelchairs. At the cross roads of footpaths, head straight across.**

Pushchairs bear right, passing the stone circle on the right, to emerge at Stormy Point. Continue from direction 16.

☺ There are many tall beech trees here, and many squirrels who love to eat the beechnuts that appear on the trees in the Autumn. Red squirrels are very rare in England now, but grey squirrels are very common. They are skilful food hunters, and often raid bird tables, hanging bags of bird nuts and even litter bins.

6. **Keep ahead and take the shallow steps to the hillock, the site of the Armada beacon, with a stone memorial at the top.**

☺ On this small hill there was once a little stone building in which fires were lit to warn when the country was being invaded. The building was hundreds of years old, and was destroyed by strong winds. A fire was lit here in 1588 to warn of a Spanish invasion. The light of the fire, and those on hilltops across the country, could be seen for miles, so that the warning soon spread. The Spaniards were defeated in a great battle at sea, and did not manage to invade.

Q: What is the date on the plaque on the site of the beacon?

A: The plaque was presented in 1961.

7.   Continue past the beacon, down through the trees towards the stone wall on the left. At the bottom, bear left along a gravel path. Pass the first set of steps and continue ahead.

(Keep close control of small children as there is a slight drop into the woods to the right of the path.)

8.   Take the second set of steps down to avoid the hazardous cliff-top path.

☺ This path passes the sandstone Edge itself. You can see it is red, but in many parts it is covered by grass, moss and lichen. There are beech trees overhanging and in places you can see their roots above the soil. The roots have to spread a long way to support them in the thin layer of soil over the rock.

In places you can see the different layers of stone on top of each other. Some people have carved their initials in the soft sandstone. Please do not do this as it wears away the rock face and looks unsightly.

9.   Climb the steps to the left, and bear left for Castle Rock.

☺ Although there were plans to build a castle at Castle Rock, it was, finally, built at Beeston in West Cheshire.

There are views over fields and farmland towards Stockport and Manchester. To the left is Manchester Airport, so you may see several planes taking off or landing.

10.   Return down the steps and bear left along the path, leading slightly downhill to the Wizard's Well. (It is a short way, on the left. Often the path is muddy.)

☺ This is the Wizard's Well. Carved in the rock above the stone basin is the face of an old man, and the words:

"Drink of this and take thy fill
For the water falls by the Wizard's will"

The legend of the Alderley Wizard has been told for hundreds of years:

The Legend of the Wizard

Long ago, a farmer was walking through the woods in the early morning. He was hoping to sell his fine, white horse at the market at Macclesfield. From amongst the trees there appeared an old man with a long, white beard. He was dressed in a dark, flowing cloak. The old man offered to buy the horse, but the farmer was greedy, and thought he would make more money at the market. He refused, and continued on his way. The old man called after him that he would get no offers for the horse, but the farmer laughed and walked on.

In the evening the farmer returned home over the Edge. He had been unable to sell the horse. As if by magic, the old man appeared from the shadows and told the farmer to follow him. He led him to an overhanging rock, where a pair of iron gates appeared from nowhere. The gates swung open and the old man led the way into a cave, going deep down into the earth. In a large cavern there were eleven white horses, all asleep, and twelve knights dressed in armour. One of the knights had no horse, so the wizard led the farmer's horse to the twelfth knight and touched its head. The horse immediately fell into a deep sleep. These twelve knights and their horses still sleep, deep within the hillside, waiting to be awakened to fight a great battle and save the country.

What of the farmer? He was rewarded with as much treasure as he could carry. Since that day, the iron gates have never been seen, though many have tried to find them. A few times people have claimed to have seen the wizard, so you never know...

11. **Soon after the Wizard's Well, follow the steps, bearing downhill. At the end of the steps, bear right along the bottom of the Edge, with a wire fence on your left. Pass a stile on the left, but continue ahead.**

☺ You may see many rabbit holes in the sandy soil. Rabbits can have six sets of young every year, with five or six rabbits born each time.

Q: Do you know the names for male and female rabbits?
A: The male is called a "buck" and the female is a "doe".

12. **The path winds between bushes and trees, then rejoins the fence. At an outcrop of holly bushes the path bears steeply uphill. Bear left at the top, keeping with the fence.**

Q: In the fields on the left there are often horses. What is a young horse called?
A: A foal.

13. **Avoid the stile to the left and continue ahead, downhill to an area of swamp. Climb the steps which lead to a T-junction. Here, go left across a small wooden footbridge, and continue a short way uphill to a well.**

☺ This is another of Alderley Edge's mysterious wells. It was supposedly put here by a farmer, who owned part of the Edge, and was jealous because his neighbour owned the part with the Wizard's Well. The basin is carved from sandstone, and the water trickles from deep inside the earth. The water overflows over the path and runs downhill, partly causing the swamp below.

14. Just to the left of the well is a path which leads uphill over exposed tree roots (not the level path a short way further to the left.) Continue to a second trough cut into rock.

☺ This is the second cause of the swamp below. To the right of the trough is a bilberry bush which has purple berries in the Summer and Autumn. The Edge would once have been covered with bushes like this.

15. Continue along the path and up the steps. The path curves to the right through the trees. Keep to the main path. At the T-junction bear left over exposed rock and tree roots to the wide sandstone plateau.

☺ This is Stormy Point. No trees grow here, partly because of all the human traffic, and partly because the ground is too rich in minerals. If you look amongst the sand and stones on the floor, you may find pieces of green stone, containing traces of copper. The miners were looking for copper which could be melted from the stone. This is called "smelting". Tools or weapons could be made from the metal.

To the right are the hills of Derbyshire and, if you look carefully, you may be able to see the tower of Lyme Cage at Lyme Park.
At Stormy Point there is a crack in the stone which is large enough to walk inside. This was once part of a mine, and is now

Scots Pines near Stormy Point

known as "The Devil's Grave". **(IT IS BARRED OFF INSIDE, SO IT IS QUITE SAFE TO ENTER.)**

16. Continue along the top of Stormy Point and follow the main path which is wide and flat, leading away through the trees, running parallel with the edge of the Cheshire Plain.

☺ There are many tall beech trees on the left which are fully grown and probably over 200 years old. Look for squirrels in the high branches, searching for beechnuts to eat. Squirrels collect nuts and bury some for Winter. Sometimes they forget where they hide their supply, so the beechnuts are left in the soil, and in the Spring some of them will begin to grow.

17. At the end, bear left just before the gate, along a path through the trees which joins a stony trackway, leading quite steeply downhill.

Pushchair Route and Escape Route: At the gate, go through the gap, pushchairs under the bar, and bear right along the trackway, which will take you back to the main car park and Wizard Tea-room.

18. Follow the trackway as it winds downhill, keeping to the main stony trackway. Various other paths and tracks lead off. At the bottom, bear right along the path, with the wire fence on your left.

☺ There are views back towards the Edge, and you can see the bare sandstone of Stormy Point. There are many different types of trees, and in the Autumn the Edge is covered with all shades of brown, yellow and red.

19. The path winds round to a small stream. Step over the stream and bear right, following the stream for a short distance, then the path bears away uphill over exposed tree roots.

☺ There are many roots across the surface of the soil here. Roots take water and food from the soil to the tree. They usually spread over a very large area, which helps to keep the tree upright.

20. The path splits into two. Bear right between the holly bushes, and keep straight ahead as the path leads uphill through an area of ferns. After this an open field comes into view on the left. Continue along the path, keeping close to the fence.

☺ This is Waterfall Wood. On the right is a steep gully with a stream running along the bottom. In very dry weather the stream dries up. This is a quieter part of Alderley Edge. Look for rabbits and squirrels.

There are fallen trees in the woods, some with fungus growing on them. Fungus can grow on dead or living wood. It often causes the death of a tree.

21. Take care on the sandstone "step" and continue along the path.

☺ On the left more sandstone can be seen, with trees growing on top and hanging over the path. The waterfall is at its best after heavy rain. In Winter it often freezes, and,instead of water, there is a column of ice.

22. **Continue past the waterfall into an area of bushes. The path emerges at a stile, bear right after the stile along a sandy farm trackway, heading gradually uphill towards farm buildings.**

☺ On the left are open fields and views to the hills, including Shuttlingsloe, which looks like an upturned basin. It is one of the highest points in Cheshire and can be seen from all over the county.

23. **Climb the stile and bear right to a further stile, after which keep left, uphill, passing the farm buildings on the left.**

Q: On the right is a brick cottage with a roof of stone. How many chimneys does it have?

A: Two.

24. **Cross the farm driveway and continue along the fenced footpath between fields, heading towards the trees of Alderley Edge. Bear left along the trackway. After a short way there is a stile on the left, leading back to the car park, or continue ahead to the Wizard Tea-room.**

Alderley Edge checklist

- [ ] A MINE SHAFT
- [ ] A DOG
- [ ] A WIZARD WITH A BEARD
- [ ] STONE STEPS
- [ ] A HOLLY BUSH
- [ ] A BLACK & WHITE COW
- [ ] A PLANE
- [ ] A HORSE'S HOOFPRINT
- [ ] A WATERFALL
- [ ] A FARMHOUSE
- [ ] SOMEONE WITH A WALKING STICK
- [ ] A FALLEN TREE

Aldford

This is a short walk (with options to make it longer) around the village of Aldford and the surrounding countryside, owned mainly by the Duke of Westminster, whose home is nearby Eaton Hall. A varied and very pleasant walk for a Sunday afternoon at any time of the year.

Starting point:	Aldford church (SJ419595) The village is well-signed from the B5130 Chester to Farndon road. If approaching from the Chester direction, bear right into the village, and there is a car park a short way along on the left, before you reach the church.
By bus:	Services between Chester and Farndon. Bus stops on the B-road just outside the village.
Distance:	A gentle 1^1/$_2$ miles (there are no escape routes). The walk can be extended by continuing further along both sides of the river, but returning the same way to continue with the circular route.
Terrain:	Mainly flat footpaths, trackways and village streets.
Maps:	OS Landranger 117
Public Toilets:	None.
Refreshments:	Pub on the main road, a short walk from the village.
Pushchairs:	Around the village only.

☺ **(IN THE VILLAGE)** This is the village of Aldford which means "old ford". A "ford" is a type of crossing place over a river, a place where the water is shallow and can be driven or waded across. At one time, there must have been a crossing here, over the River Dee, which runs nearby.

Looking around, you can see that most of the houses are similar, built of brick with diamond patterns below the bedroom windows. Some of the houses have square chimneys and some have round ones.
This village, and several others in the area, **(SAIGHTON, ECCLESTON AND PULFORD)** are estate villages of Eaton Hall, which is on the other side of the river. This means they belonged to the hall, and the villagers would have to pay rent for their homes. Eaton Hall is the home of the Duke of Westminster. Duke is a title which is passed on, so that when one Duke dies, the eldest son will then become the next Duke. There have been many Dukes of Westminster living here. The first Duke had this village built nearly 150 years ago. More houses were added a hundred years ago. Can you see any plaques with dates?

1.   **Enter the churchyard via the main gates, opposite the village post office.**

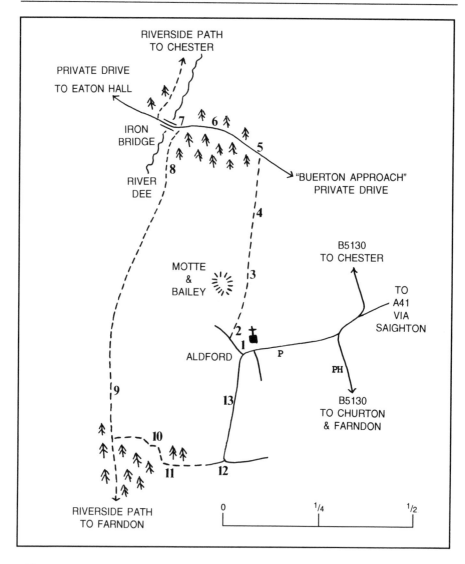

😊 This is the church of Saint John the Baptist. It has a sandstone tower with a spire. There is also a strange, smaller tower, attached to the side of the main tower, with tiny windows. This has stairs inside which lead to the bells. If you look up at the main tower, you will see what looks like an arched window. It has no glass, but there are strips of wood. The bells are inside here, and the gaps between the wooden strips let out the sound. They also let birds and bats in. Bats are like winged mice, and many people are frightened of them, though they are quite harmless. They are "nocturnal" animals which means they only come out at night, when it's dark. During the day they sleep, hanging upside down in the roofs of barns, old buildings and church towers.

Q: Can you find the tallest monument at the front of the church? It is in memory of one of the Dukes of Westminster. When was it restored?

A: 1901, as it says at the end of the plaque.

Just to the left of the church door there is an old sundial. This was used for telling the time. The sun casts a shadow on the "clockface", and the shadow moves throughout the day. You will have noticed that the sun seems to move in the sky. It rises in the east in the morning, and sets in the west at night. That is why it may be sunny in your bedroom in the morning, but not in the afternoon, or vice versa.

2. **Bear to the left of the tower to a set of steps, leading over the wall. Take the white wooden gate on the immediate right and follow the path ahead across the field, to the right of the earthwork.**

On the left is a huge bank and ditch which was once part of a "motte and bailey", which was a sort of castle. It was built long before the village. The bank and ditch were for protection. Neighbouring villagers weren't always very friendly, and may have tried to steal your land or belongings. The Welsh border is nearby, and Welsh robbers would also come and take whatever they could. On the "island" in the middle of the ditch, there would have been wooden buildings, and the ditch would have been full of water. It is very old, and was built at least 800 years ago.

Near the castle there is a large oak tree which must also be old, because its trunk is very wide. It is hollow inside, but still alive. If you are small enough you could crawl inside and stand up.

3. **Continue along the path, passing the earthwork on the left, and go through the gate. Keep straight ahead across the field.**

In the distance ahead, you should be able to see a very tall tower rising over the treetops, which looks like the top of a rocket. It is, in fact, the clocktower of the chapel at Eaton Hall, the home of the Duke of Westminster. It is 175 feet (over 50 metres) high, which is very high, even for a church steeple.

4. **Go through the metal gate and head for the bottom right corner of the field.**

You should be able to see a black and white house ahead in the distance which you will come to later. You can probably see black and white cows in the fields around you. Even if there are no cows here, there may be cowpats on the ground, which tell you that they have been here! There are often brown flies on cowpats which are called "dung flies". They eat the cowpat and lay their eggs in it.

5.   Go through the wooden gate, and bear left along the concrete driveway.

😊 On both sides there are woods, with many different trees, such as sycamore and oak. Acorns are the fruit of the oak tree. You have probably seen them many times before. At one time they were collected and fed to pigs. Today they can be roasted and ground to make a coffee-like drink. The wood from the oak tree is very strong and was often used for building the frames of houses.

There are also rhododendron bushes in the woods which have colourful flowers in the Spring and Summer. They do not lose their dark green, oval leaves in the Winter, so they are called "evergreens", because they are green all the year round. Another familiar evergreen is holly. There are several holly bushes in the woods, some having red berries in the Autumn. A short way ahead, look for another evergreen, a tall tree called a "yew". It has a soft, flaky bark and dark green leaves which are small and thin, like needles. Like holly, many yews have red berries, which are poisonous. Can you spot a yew tree?

6.   Keep left to the bridge.

😊 This bridge is made of iron, a metal, and it crosses the River Dee, which flows through the city of Chester, and then to the sea. The bridge was built in 1824 to carry one of the many long driveways to Eaton Hall. The two men responsible for building the bridge were William Hazledean and William Stuttle. Can you find their names on the bridge?

On the opposite bank is the black and white building you could see across the fields. Only the top half of the house is black and white. The bottom half is built of brick. It is part of the Eaton Hall estate, and has the same diamond patterns in the brickwork as many of the houses in the village.

(To extend the route it is permissible to cross the bridge, where a footpath leads off to the right, through the trees, and follows the river to the estate village of Eccleston, then on towards Chester. Return the same way to the bridge and continue with the route.)

7.   Bear left, directly before the bridge, along a signed footpath which runs close to the river.

😊 There are more yew trees along the path at this point.

8.   Climb the stile and continue straight ahead. The path runs along the river bank, but frequently zigzags to the edge of the field when the river bank is impassable. Keep as close to the river as possible.

😊 You should be able to see the tall spire of the church, across the fields.

Estate Housing, Aldford

Occasionally, you should be able to see the river, but sometimes, it will be hidden by the tall plants that grow on the bank. There are nettles which can sting, and prickly thistles which have purple flowering heads in the Summer. Next time you have any pound coins, look at them, as some show a thistle on one side. The thistle is the "emblem" of Scotland. An emblem is a picture which is used as a sort of badge. The leek is the emblem of Wales, and the red rose is the emblem of England.

Q: Look for a sign, almost hidden by the tall plants. What is the speed limit for boats on the water?

A: 6 mph, or 6 miles per hour.

☺ A little way ahead there is a farm, over on the left, and you can probably see the church steeple above it. There is a haybarn, which in the Autumn and Winter should be full of hay. Hay is a tall grass which is grown for winter food for cows and horses.

There are several willow trees close to the river and there are many more on the other side which lean right over the water. Can you recognise them? Willows have long, narrow, oval-shaped leaves and the lower branches used to be collected to make baskets.

9. Continue along the river bank for some way, to the end of the field, where there is an area of fenced woodland with a stile leading over. Do not cross the stile, instead bear left, with the woods on your right.

(The path continues for some way along the river and makes an interesting extension to this short walk, but return the same way to this point and follow the return directions.)

10. After a short way, bear right over a makeshift stile next to a gate, and follow the path to a farm trackway. Bear left.

☺ There are high hedges on both sides of the trackway. It contains wild plants like prickly hawthorns, and a climbing plant which has started to cover the other bushes. Along the grassy banks you may see rabbit burrows, or larger holes made by badgers, with piles of soft sand outside the entrance. The badgers have scraped this out with their strong claws. Badgers, like bats, are nocturnal, they only come out at night, so it is unlikely you will see one.

11. Keep straight ahead, avoiding all other trackways. Go through the five-barred gate and continue ahead.

Q: There is a weathervane on top of a building on the right. A weathervane points in the direction the wind is blowing. What animal is on this one?

A: A bird, probably a grouse.

12. Bear left along the quiet village street.

Q: The first houses on the left are a pair of semi-detached cottages. "Semi-detached" means there are two houses joined together. They are the most common type of houses in towns and cities. These cottages are built of plain bricks, and there are dates over the doors which tell you when they were built. What is the date?

A: 1859.

☺ This is School Lane, and, not surprisingly, there was once a school here. Perhaps you can tell which was the school building?

Q: Look out on the left for the old "thatched" cottage; that is a house with a roof made from reeds, which is how most roofs would be made at one time. There is a model bird sitting in the middle of the roof. How many tall chimneys are there on the cottage?

A: Four.

☺ You will pass other semi-detached cottages, with dates of 1856 and 1858. As you may have noticed by now, most of the village was built around the 1850s, though there are a few houses which are older.

Ahead is the church tower, the end of the walk.

13. **Bear right to the church/starting point and car park.**

Aldford checklist

- [ ] A "WEATHERVANE"
- [ ] A BLACK AND WHITE COW
- [ ] A TELEPHONE BOX
- [ ] A TRACTOR
- [ ] AN IRON BRIDGE
- [ ] A WHITE GATE
- [ ] A BLACK AND WHITE COTTAGE
- [ ] A POST BOX
- [ ] A STINGING NETTLE
- [ ] A RABBIT HOLE
- [ ] A HOLLY BUSH
- [ ] A DOG

𝓐udlem

Audlem is a pleasant, small town in South Cheshire, and close by is the Shropshire Union Canal, well known for its frequent locks, of which there are 15 in the immediate area. The surrounding countryside is relatively flat; an attractive patchwork of hedged fields and pastures. This route takes in the town, the countryside and the canal. A very rewarding half day walk, or longer if you include a picnic stop. (There are picnic tables at certain points along the canal.)

Starting point:	Car park in the centre of the village, (SJ659437) well-signed, just off Cheshire Street/A529. From the main village street, turn off by the church, and the car park is a short way on the left.
By bus:	Services from Crewe and Nantwich to village centre.
Distance:	Entire route: just under 6 miles Shorter route: 3 miles
Terrain:	Almost entirely flat paths through pleasant, farmed fields and along the canal towpath. A short distance along lanes.
Maps:	OS Landranger 118
Public Toilets:	In the car park/starting point (there is a nominal entrance charge!) including disabled facilities.
Refreshments:	Pubs, cafes etc in village
Pushchairs:	Not suitable, except along canal towpath.

1. **From the car park, bear right along Cheshire Street, towards the centre of the village.**

Q: What animal is the pub named after?

A: A lamb.

2. **Carefully cross the road and climb the steps to the church.**

☺ This is Saint James's Church and the oldest parts are between seven and eight hundred years old. It is built of local sandstone, and, if you look carefully, you can see where some of the large, square sandstone blocks have been replaced as they became worn and damaged. The church is built on a slight hill, and from the surrounding countryside the tower can be seen rising above the roofs of the little town.

Q: In which year was the clock "installed" in the tower?

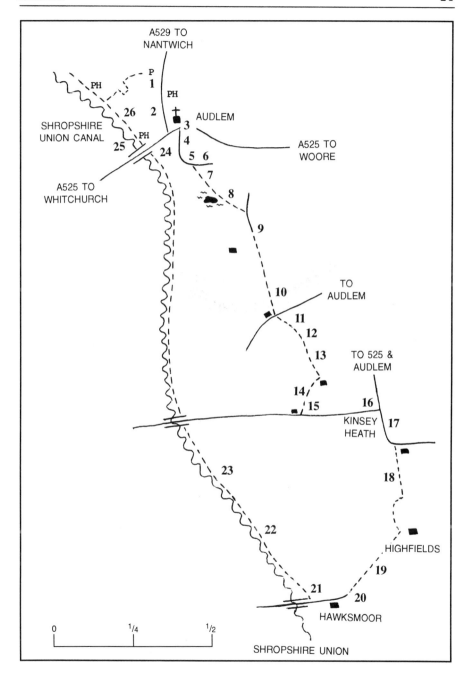

A529 TO
NANTWICH

P
PH
1
PH

26　2
SHROPSHIRE
UNION CANAL
PH
25　24

AUDLEM
3
4
5　6
7

A525 TO
WOORE

A525 TO
WHITCHURCH

8

9

TO
AUDLEM

10
11
12

13

TO 525 &
AUDLEM

14
15

16
17

KINSEY
HEATH

18

23

HIGHFIELDS

22

19

21

20

HAWKSMOOR

0　　　　¼　　　　½

SHROPSHIRE UNION

A: There is a plaque on the tower which will give you the answer. The clock was
      installed for the "coronation", or crowning, of King George V and Queen
      Mary, on 22 June, 1911.

3.   Go down the steps to the main gates of the church.

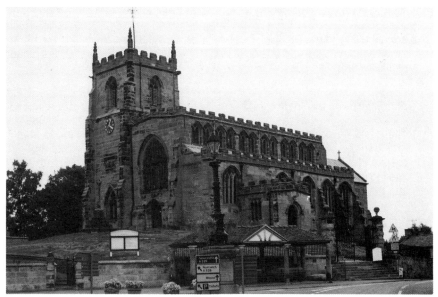

The Church

☺   At the bottom of the steps is a building which looks like, and is now, a bus
    shelter, but it used to be the town's butter market, and was built in 1733.

4.   Cross the main village street and go down the narrow road (Vicarage Lane),
      directly opposite the church.

(On the left is the Old Priest House Coffee Shop, a suitable place for a
refreshment stop, if you feel you've earned it!)

5.   Follow the lane downhill. It soon curves to the left, after which take the
      footpath off to the right, over the grass. Cross over the stream.

☺   On the right, just before the bridge, there is a row of lime trees which have
    large, heart-shaped leaves. Audlem gets its name from this type of tree. The
    town was originally known as "Alda's Lime". Alda was a person, and, over the
    years, the name has been shortened and changed slightly, to become Audlem.

6.   Go over the bridge and keep straight ahead, climbing to the top of the grassy
      hill.

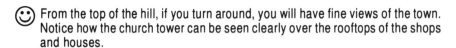 From the top of the hill, if you turn around, you will have fine views of the town. Notice how the church tower can be seen clearly over the rooftops of the shops and houses.

7. **Continue straight ahead.**

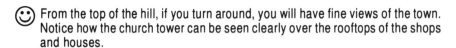 You should pass a swamp or marshy area on the right, with many reeds and bulrushes around its edges. Bulrushes have brown, cigar-shaped "pods" which are full of tiny seeds. In the springtime the pods burst and the seeds are blown away, so that they may find some soil and begin to grow. Bulrushes like clean, shallow water, like this.

8. **Continue to the stile in the far right corner of the field. Bear left, then right along the main trackway, soon passing between buildings. Continue ahead.**

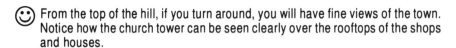 There is a haybarn on the right, in which the farmer will store hay, to stop it rotting in the Winter. Hay is tall grass which can be used for winter food for cows and horses. In the late Summer you may see hay being cut and made into big rolls. It is then left in the sun to dry for several days, before it is brought into the barns.

9. **When the drive bears to the right, keep straight ahead along a rough trackway, between fields.**

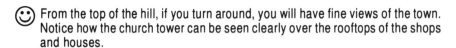 In the Autumn, the trees and bushes have many berries which carry their seeds. Towards the end of the trackway there is a hedgerow with several plants that have brightly-coloured fruit or berries. If it is late Summer or Autumn, see if you can spot any. Damsons are purple plums, a little bigger than a marble. Hawthorns have sharp thorns and small, blood-red berries. Rosehips are orangey-red and look like small tomatoes.

10. **Climb the stile and take the footpath directly over the lane.**

Escape Route: Bear right along the lane, and right at the junction. Continue to the canal. Take the gate on the left before the bridge, and bear right along the towpath. Continue with the route from direction 24.

Q: What is the name of the cottage on the lane, to the right of the stile?
A: "Holly Cottage".

11. **Follow the path straight ahead, with the hedge on your right.**

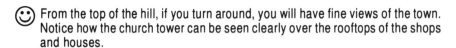 Again, there are many berries in the hedgerows. These can be eaten by birds and small animals through the cold Winter, when there is little else to eat, but don't you eat any! Even if there is snow, the berries are brightly-coloured and can easily be found.

Some birds "migrate" in the winter. This means they fly away to other countries where it is warmer, like Africa. Some birds stay here and brave the cold. Sparrows and robins can be seen all year. They need a lot to eat in the winter to keep them alive, so why not put some food out for them at home, especially nuts, which contain fat to keep the birds warm.

12. **After a short way the path bears left across the middle of the field to a stile. (If you miss the path, continue around the edge of the field and you will eventually arrive at the stile.)**

13. **Cross the stile and continue straight ahead, keeping to the edge of the field. At the end of the field the path bears to the right in front of a house. A short way after the house take the stile on the left. Bear diagonally right.**

☺ Here is another small pond. In the Summer it is surrounded by yellow flowers which attract butterflies and other insects, like dragonflies, which are often bright blue with long wings and thin bodies. They may be seen hovering close to the surface of the water.

Q: Butterflies lay their eggs on leaves. When they hatch, it isn't a butterfly that crawls out. Do you know what it is?

A: A caterpillar. Caterpillars eat as many green leaves as they can, then they make themselves a "cocoon" or "chrysalis", which is a sort of small, furry egg. Inside the cocoon they begin to change, and, when they finally emerge, they have grown wings and become a butterfly.

14. **Pass the pond on the right and continue ahead to a stile in the hedge. Cross the field to a further stile in the right corner.**

☺ In the field there is an old bath which cows drink from. A thirsty cow can drink up to a bathful of water every day!

Q: Next to the stile **(ON THE RIGHT)** is "Kinsey House". What is the date on the front of the building?

A: 1902.

Escape Route: To cut the route in half, bear right along the lane. Avoid the turning to the right and continue ahead to the canal. Go through the gate on the left, before the bridge. Bear right along the towpath, continuing with direction 24.

15. **Bear left along the lane. Avoid the footpath to the right and continue to the T-junction.**

Q: You should soon pass a row of brick cottages. One of them is named after a flower, and one is named after a tree. What are their names?

A: "Rose Cottage" and "Oak Cottage".

Q: Further on there is a black and white metal road sign next to a post box. How far are Audlem and Nantwich from here?

A: As it says on the sign, Audlem is 1 mile and Nantwich is 8 miles away.

16. **Bear right along Woodhouse Lane.**

Q: After a short way there is a gate on the left, and a driveway lined with tall pine trees, leading to a house. What is its name?

A: The unusual name can be found on the gate. "Kynsal Lodge".

17. **Soon, the lane begins to bear to the left. On the corner there is a black and white house. Take the unsigned driveway directly before the house, crossing the cattle grid, and continuing ahead.**

☺ Over on the left is a mixed woodland, of many different types of trees which are very colourful in the Autumn. In the fields there will probably be cows grazing. They pull the grass up with their strong, rough tongues and seem to chew almost all the time.

18. **When the driveway splits, bear right. Continue to a cattle grid, after which the drive begins to bear to the left. Here, bear right through an open gateway between wire fences and keep straight ahead towards a metal gate in the far right corner of the field.**

☺ Over on the left is a large house, with a wooden frame and white panels, and many tall, brick chimneys. It is called "Highfields" and was built in 1615.

19. **Go through the metal gate and keep straight ahead along a clear, rutted trackway.**

☺ Here there are large, open fields which may have crops such as wheat, corn, potatoes or green vegetables like cabbage. You may see a tractor ploughing the field, if it is Autumn, or spreading seeds, if it is Spring. In the late Summer you may see a farmer "harvesting" or collecting the crop, using tractors and other machines. At one time the crops had to be collected by hand, and it was a very long job.

20. **Keep straight ahead. The track becomes a concrete driveway and leads towards farm buildings. Keep straight ahead between the barns and farmhouse, and continue along the lane.**

Q: Look for the farmhouse on the left, after the barns. How many chimneys are there on the main roof?

A: Three.

21. A short way along the lane you will come to a canal bridge. Go through the gate on the right, before the bridge, down the steps and bear right along the towpath.

☺ If you look back at the bridge, you will see that it is made of brick, but it has been painted white. It is easier for people on canal boats to see it in the evening, so they won't crash into it, or stand up and bang their heads! Can you see any boats on the water?

The water is almost chocolate-coloured. When the canals were built, they were dug out by men with spades, as there were no diggers in those days. The bottom and sides of the canal were then lined with a thick clay, which is watertight, so the water could not sink into the soil. It is the clay that has coloured the water.

There are many wild plants growing along the path, like nettles, which can sting you. There are also thistles, which are quite tall and prickly, with purple flowers. There is hogweed, which is also tall, and has clusters of white flowers in the Spring and Summer.

Q: Soon you will come across another bridge. All the bridges along the canal are numbered. What number is this one?

A: There should be a sign on one side above the arch. This is number 73.

22. Pass under the bridge and continue along the towpath.

☺ After the bridge there is a sandy bank alongside the path, with many blackberry bushes and hawthorns growing. Can you see any holes in the bank? The smaller ones will be rabbit burrows. The larger holes with piles of sand outside them are likely to have been made by badgers. You have probably never seen a living badger, as they are "nocturnal" animals, which means they usually come out at night. They have black and white heads, and greyish bodies. A badger hole is called a "sett". It is usually made up of many long, linked tunnels, with several different entrances. Badgers, unlike many wild animals, live in family groups, even when they are fully grown.

A little further on, there are views across the water to the fields on the other side, where you may see horses grazing.

Q: Look out for an old black and white signpost, alongside the path. The one you saw earlier was for people using the road. This one is for people using the canal. How far is it to Nantwich from here?

A: 8 miles, which is the same as on the road sign.

23. Pass under all subsequent bridges and continue ahead.

There are now trees on both sides of the canal, shading the water. They are mainly sycamores, which you may recognise. They are quite common in parks and gardens.

Notice the metal rings in the ground where boats can be tied up. Perhaps there are some boats to see. Canal boats are called "narrow boats" because they are long and narrow. Some people live on narrow boats, but usually they are used for boating holidays.

Further along you will come to the first of the canal "locks". A "lock" is a kind of "lift" for boats. The canal is moving downhill towards the flat Cheshire Plain, and the locks are like a series of steps which lower the narrow boats gently up or downhill. If you are lucky, you may see one of them in use. (**THE BEST TIME IS A SUMMER AFTERNOON AT THE WEEK-END.**) There are no less than 15 locks along this part of the canal, so you will pass many more of them before the end of the walk.

Soon there are several more locks. Notice, as you pass, that the water after each lock is lower than the water before it, as the canal heads downhill towards the Plain. The locks can hold two boats at a time. There may also be colourful boats tied up along the canal, some will have names painted on them.

Look for the numbers on the bridges as you go under them.

24. **When nearly in Audlem, there are houses on the right. Go under the road bridge (78).**

 The pub high on the right is called "The Bridge Inn". It has been a pub for many years, and was always popular with the boatmen. It still is!

25. **Climb the steps on the right to Audlem Mill canal shop, then continue towards "The Shroppie Fly" inn.**

 (**AT THE CANAL SHOP**) This building is now a shop selling everything for canal boats and boating holidays. At one time it was a mill, grinding grain, like wheat, into flour which could then be made into bread. The canal would have been used to bring the grain to the mill, and then take sacks of flour to other towns to sell to bakeries.

Further ahead is a pub called the "Shroppie Fly". The name has nothing to do with flies. "Fly Boats" were fast boats for carrying people, and "Shroppie" is a local nickname for the canal, which is properly called the "Shropshire Union Canal". The pub was once a warehouse, storing goods brought by the canal. Notice it still has a crane outside. This was used for hauling heavy sacks of coal or potatoes on and off the boats.

26. **Head into the car park of "The Shroppie Fly" and bear right. In the back right corner there are a set of steps leading uphill into the trees. Follow the path to the sports field, and cross to the car park and starting point.**

Audlem checklist

☐ A CHURCH TOWER

☐ A POST BOX

☐ A COW

☐ A TRACTOR

☐ A RABBIT OR HARE

☐ A BIRD'S FEATHER

☐ A POND

☐ A CANAL BOAT

☐ A CRANE OR WINCH

☐ A HORSE

☐ BERRIES ON A TREE (or blossom in spring)

☐ A BRICK BRIDGE

Barthomley

Barthomley is a quiet village in the south-east of the county. During the civil war, the villagers barricaded themselves in the church tower, but were smoked out by the king's men. Twelve were executed. The church, and this violent event, appear in Alan Garner's novel, "Red Shift".

The surrounding countryside is rural and largely unspoiled, apart from the distant sound of the motorway.

Starting point:	The church of Saint Bertoline, Barthomley. (SJ767524). Car parking space along the lane, near to the White Lion inn, or at the front entrance to the church. Barthomley is close to junction 16 of the M6 and is well-signed. Take the B5078, and then the first left turning which will take you straight into the village.
Buses:	From Crewe. Stops in the village.
Distance:	Entire route: 3 miles
Terrain:	Mainly flat footpaths across farmed fields.
Maps:	OS Landranger 118
Refreshments:	The White Lion inn, Barthomley
Pushchairs:	Unsuitable

☺ **(FROM THE DRIVEWAY IN FRONT OF THE CHURCH)** This is the Church of Saint Bertoline. It was built several hundred years ago, but was restored in the last century. It was built on a slight hill overlooking the village, so that its tower could be seen from miles away. A spirit of a dog is supposed to run close to the church after sunset. To see it, supposedly brings bad luck.

1. From the church, continue up the hill, passing the driveway to "The Rectory" on the right, and continue along the hedge to a small pond.

☺ Hidden away in the trees is a small, muddy pond, with many reeds growing on the far side. This quiet spot gives shelter and water for birds, which you may hear scuttling away between the undergrowth. Some of the trees have ivy growing on them. Ivy is a climbing plant, with tiny "suckers" which help it cling to walls or the bark of trees. It can cover whole areas of woodland. The leaves stay green all year and are often used in Christmas decorations.

2. The path rounds the pond to a stile on the right. Cross the stile, and bear left to a further stile, taking you into open fields.

☺ The woods on the left contain many different types of tree, including willows which like damp ground. There are also elderberry trees which have clusters

of small black berries in the late Summer and Autumn. See how many trees
you can recognise.

3. Continue straight across the field, slightly uphill, to a further stile in a hedge,
    towards the right corner of the field.

☺ Are there any ducks on the small pond in the middle of the field?

4. Continue straight ahead, again there is a slight climb towards the end of the
    field. The stile is to the right of an iron gate. Continue straight across the
    field.

5. The next stile can be found to the right of the two water troughs. Continue
    ahead.

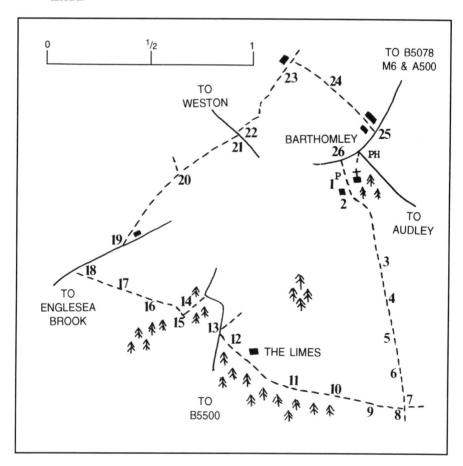

☺ There are rabbit holes in the sandy bank near to the stile. Rabbits live in family groups. Their holes are called "burrows", or together are called a "warren". Rabbits eat grass, leaves and green shoots.

6. **This smaller field drops slightly to the next stile, after which the path climbs gently, with a hawthorn hedge on the left.**

☺ Over on the right is a farm called "The Limes". Perhaps the field you are walking through has been planted with a crop, such as wheat or corn. Wheat is tall, like yellow grass. Corn is even taller, with long green leaves. Can you think of any food that is made from wheat or corn?

7. **Climb the steps to the stile, and this time bear right to a further stile.**

☺ At about this point you will be crossing the border from Cheshire into the neighbouring county of Staffordshire. (Does it look any different?)

8. **Cross the stile and bear diagonally left up the hill.**

☺ From the top of the hill there are views over the mainly flat, farming countryside. In some places the fields are wide and open, rather than small and surrounded by colourful hedgerows. This is because trees and hedgerows have been chopped down so that it is easier for the farmer to use modern machines to plough, plant and collect the crops. Unfortunately, this means that the homes of many animals, birds and insects are destroyed.

The country was once completely covered with trees, except for the very highest mountains. Over thousands of years, people have cut down the trees for wood, or to make fields for farming, or space for building. There are now very few areas covered with woodland.
If you look carefully, you may be able to see the top of the church tower.

9. **At the stile the arrow points diagonally left, but the next stile is actually straight across the field, slightly downhill. Do not cross the stile, but bear right along the hedgerow.**

☺ Through the bushes and trees you can see water below, with floating weeds, and many trees and brambles surrounding it. The pool is not natural, but has been made by damming the stream, which is called Dean Brook.

About now you will be passing over the border again, back into Cheshire.

10. **A stile in the corner of the field leads down into the woods. Cross the bridge and follow the steps up to the stile. Continue ahead with the woods on your left.**

☺ Again, these are mixed woodlands, with elderberry trees with their Autumn clusters of dark berries and oak trees which provide acorns for squirrels in Winter. On the ground between the trees there are ferns which grow well here.

11. **Keep the woods on your left and cross various stiles in close succession, heading towards the farm buildings.**

Q: This is "Limes Farm" again. How many chimney pots can you count on the farmhouse?

A: Five.

12. **After the farm, the path passes a small stream on the left. Shortly after this, bear away from the woods, across the field towards the stile in the hedgerow. Bear right along the lane.**

Escape Route: To return to the starting point, bear right along the driveway of "Limes Farm", and take the footpath immediately on the left, which will lead you back across the fields to the church.

13. **Continue along the lane for a short distance. There is a narrow grass verge for most of the way. Take the footpath off to the left.**

Escape Route: Continue along the lane and bear right at the junction, which will take you back to Barthomley.

14. **Follow the path through the area of woodland. Keep to the main path.**

☺ Again there are many oak trees, blackberries and ferns. There are small bogs on either side of the path. Make sure you don't fall in!

15. **Cross the bridge and stile, and bear right to a further stile and bridge, then bear left along the edge of the field. At the corner, head right along the edge of the woodland.**

16. **If there is a crop growing in the field this part of the path may be difficult to follow. Do not continue along the woods as far as the edge of the field. Instead, bear right across the field towards a clump of trees.**

☺ These trees surround an area of swamp. There are elderberry trees and several crab apple trees. These have very small apples, about the size of large cherries. They are very bitter and can give you stomach ache, so don't try eating one!

17. **Continue across the field to the next clump of trees.**

☺ Here there is a small pond with lilies floating on the water. Nettles, dock (tall, with large oval leaves) and rosebay willow herb which has pink flowers, grow around its edges.

18. **Continue ahead. In the left corner of the field there is a stile. Cross this, and bear right along the hedge to the lane. Bear right along the lane, passing a farm driveway on the left.**

Q: On your right, there is a high hedge, made mainly out of a plant that has dark green, prickly leaves. What is it called?

A: Holly. It is often used as part of Christmas decorations because it stays green all year and some types have bright red berries in the winter. You may have heard the Christmas carol, "The Holly and the Ivy". Ivy also stays green all year round.

19. Take the trackway off to the left, directly before the next house. It passes behind the house and then between fields.

☺ This is a "bridleway" which means it can be used by horses. You may see horses' hoofprints or shoe prints in the ground. See which is the largest print you can find.

20. Avoid the footpath to the left and continue ahead.

☺ There are often horses grazing in the fields along this path. Over on the right you should be able to see the back of a farm **(OLD HALL FARM)** and, if you look carefully, you may see the tower of the church over the treetops.

21. Carefully cross the lane and take the stile opposite.

Escape Route: Bear right along the lane and then left at the junction, which will take you back to the village.

22. From the stile, head across the field and over the small stream, aiming to the right of the houses. Follow the edge of the field, with the hedge on your left.

☺ You may be able to hear the sound of the main roads again. On the right, are the houses of the village of Barthomley, and on the left, are a couple of old brick barns which have stable doors, so that the top part could be left open for the horses to see out.

23. You should come to a stile on the left. Do not cross the stile, but bear right, straight across the field towards the church.

24. On the other side of the field, take the stile and follow the path which leads between attractive cottages and the village bowling green. Keep straight ahead, which will bring you to the village. Bear right along the pavement.

☺ In the hedge on the right is a well; water runs from a pipe into a stone trough. You can see the water is very clear.

Q: Like many of the houses in Barthomley, the village inn is black and white. What is it called?

A: "The White Lion".

The White Lion Inn

25. **Carefully cross the road and climb the church steps.**

☺ In the churchyard there are several yew trees. Can you spot one?. They have small, dark green leaves; flaky reddish-brown bark and, sometimes, red berries.

26. **Cross the graveyard to return to the church car park and starting point.**

Barthomley checklist

- [ ] A CHURCH TOWER
- [ ] A POND WITH REEDS
- [ ] A BLACK AND WHITE COTTAGE
- [ ] A GRAVESTONE
- [ ] A BLACK AND WHITE COW
- [ ] A RABBIT
- [ ] A BIRD'S FEATHER
- [ ] A TRACTOR
- [ ] A HORSE
- [ ] A STREAM
- [ ] A FIELD OF WHEAT OR CORN
- [ ] A DOG

Big Mere and Marbury

This Marbury is near to Whitchurch –, not the one near Northwich. This is an attractive village, overlooking Big Mere and the gentle hills that rise towards the Shropshire border. Good views, a large resident wildfowl population and a stroll along the canal bank make this a varied and very pleasant walk.

Starting point:	Lay-by at Willey Moor on the A49, a couple of miles north of Whitchurch (SJ539466)
By rail:	The nearest station is at Whitchurch, 2 miles to the south
Distance:	Entire route, 6 miles
Terrain:	Canal towpaths and footpaths over some hilly areas
Maps:	OS Landranger 117
Public Toilets:	No public toilets. Facilities at two pubs for patrons only
Refreshments:	Pubs
Pushchairs:	A mile each way along the towpath. The rest of the route is unsuitable

1. **From the lay-by, head for the bridge that crosses over the canal. On the right side of the road there is a narrow path, leading down to the canal. Bear right along the towpath.**

☺ This is part of the Shropshire Union Canal. There are canals all over the country. They are man-made waterways which were built for moving goods from one place to another.

Boats are tied to the metal posts along the path so that they don't float away. Canal boats are long and are called "narrow boats". Some people live on them, but most are used for holidays.
Very soon you should come across the first "lock". **(QUOISLEY LOCK.)** The land isn't always flat, and sometimes a canal goes from high country to low country, and a lock is used to lower or raise a boat. If you look at the level of the water on each side of the lock, you will see that one side is higher than the other. If you are lucky, you may see a boat using the lock **(WEEKEND AFTERNOONS ARE USUALLY THE BEST TIME)** and you will see how it works. There is no electricity involved. It works by the power of the water.

Q: The hedgerow along the path is made up of many different plants. Some of these plants have blossom in the spring and berries in the autumn. Can you recognise any of them?

A: Elderberries are small and black. Rosehips are red, and about the size of cherries. Hawthorn berries are red, but smaller.

☺ Along the path you will have to walk between prickly thistles and tall reeds.

You will soon come to another lock, next to a pub, which was once a lock-keeper's cottage and stable block, where horses slept. It is a popular stopping place for the people on the canal, so you may see a long line of boats tied up here, perhaps for the night. Near the pub you will have to cross over the canal.

(This is Willeymoor Lock, and the pub is "Willeymoor Lock Tavern". There are seats outside and a family room.)

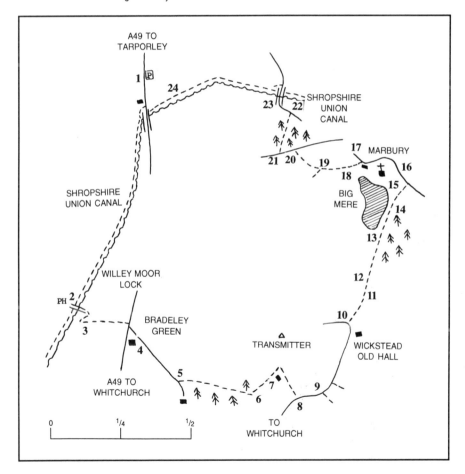

2. At the pub, cross the bridge over the canal. Follow the path back towards the canal, alongside the overflow for a short way, to a stile off to the left.

3. Keep close to the hedge on the left, and continue towards the road. Climb the stile and carefully cross the road. Bear right for a short way, and then left down Bradeley Green Lane.

Q: There is a "T" sign at the start of this lane. You have probably seen signs like this quite often, especially in the town, but do you know what it means?

A: It means the road is a dead end and doesn't go anywhere for cars.

☺ On the right is a wildfowl "sanctuary". This is a place where injured birds stay, because they may not be able to look after themselves in the wild. You should be able to see or hear ducks, geese and other water birds around a pond, surrounded by wire fencing to keep them safe from wild animals. Ducks and geese can fly or swim. They can even swim underwater. Their feathers are coated in a natural oil which keeps them warm and "waterproof".

4. The lane continues uphill, past the farm buildings. Follow the main track, then, as it bears to the right to a house, keep straight ahead along a grassy pathway.

☺ There are high hedges on both sides of the path. This is a bridleway which means it is also used by horses. Look out for hoofprints in the mud. Further ahead you will probably also see deep tractor marks in the trackway. Branches hang over and cut out some of the light. Look for ivy growing on the tree trunks. Ivy is a climbing plant and will grow on almost anything. It has tiny suckers with which it can attach itself to trees and walls.

5. The path soon joins a farmer's trackway. Keep straight ahead, slightly uphill.

☺ Beneath the hedges there are sandy banks which have many rabbit holes. Rabbits dig their holes under trees or hedges because the roots help to support the roofs of their burrows, and stop them falling in. There are also holes dug by badgers. These are called "setts", and are often slightly larger than rabbit holes. Badgers scrape out the soil or sand from inside, and leave it piled up outside the entrance to the holes. They are "nocturnal" creatures, which means that they usually come out at night, so it is not very likely that you will see one.

6. Keep ahead until you come across a well-signed footpath off to the left. Go through the gate and follow the path.

☺ After a short way you should pass a small pond on the left, surrounded by reeds and overhanging trees. There is also an unusual plant growing here, which likes the moist soil. It is very tall and has huge leaves like umbrellas. It is related to the "rhubarb" plant.

Q: When you pass the house on the right, can you count how many chimney pots there are on the roof?

A: Eight.

☺ Straight ahead, there is a metal tower in a field. This is an aerial and it can pick up radio signals. You will be able to see it from many places along the rest of the walk.

7. **Follow the track round to the right, passing the house.**

Q: There are stables at the back of the house, so you may see some horses. Horses have long "hair" on their heads and down their necks. What is this called?

A: A "mane". Other animals have "manes" as well, such as male lions.

8. **Bear left along the quiet lane.**

☺ Can you spot a house with large butterflies on its walls. **(ON THE RIGHT.)** If it is Summer or Autumn, see if you can spot any fruit trees, such as apples, or damsons, which are small, dark purple plums.

9. **Avoid the first two footpaths to the right. Keep to the lane.**

☺ You should soon pass a triangular sign with a picture of old people. Triangular road signs are usually warnings. This one warns drivers to take care, as there may be old people along the lane. An old people's home is on the right. **(WICKSTEAD OLD HALL)**

Escape Route: Follow the lane for a mile. Take the footpath off to the left after Quoisley Hall, then continue from direction 21.

10. **Take the next footpath on the right, after Wickstead Old Hall. Follow the path downhill, with the hedge on the right.**

☺ This is about the half way point of the walk, and from here, there are views for miles over the fertile Cheshire countryside.

11. **Climb the stile and bear diagonally right, downhill, heading to the right of the lake, visible ahead, and to the left of the woodlands.**

☺ Below you should be able to see some water, which is called Big Mere, and also a church tower. You are heading in this direction.

12. **Climb the next stile and continue straight ahead, across the field, following the "valley" in the middle.**

☺ There are many different trees in the woods on your right, including prickly hawthorns, poplars and silver birch, named for their silver-white bark.

13. **Climb the stile in the bottom right corner of the field, and follow the path along the water's edge.**

☺ There are many reeds and waterside plants which provide food and shelter for water insects, such as dragonflies and water beetles. In Spring and Summer there are pink and yellow flowers along the water's edge. In March, look for frog spawn which is like a clear jelly, usually around the stems of reeds. Inside the jelly are hundreds of eggs which will hatch into tadpoles. (Don't try to eat any.)

Q: Do you know what tadpoles grow into?

A: They lose their tails, grow legs and become frogs.

14. **Climb the stile and keep along the side of the lake to the next stile, then bear diagonally right.**

☺ There will almost certainly be ducks and geese on the water. Big Mere is a very popular place with them. Ducks and geese "moult" in summer, which means that some of their feathers come out, so they can keep cooler in the warm weather. Look out for feathers on the grass. The feathers will grow back as the weather becomes colder. Dogs and cats also moult. We just wear fewer clothes!

15. **Cross the field to the gate, and bear left along the lane.**

☺ Overlooking the lake is the church of Saint Michael. Like many churches it was built on a slight hill, so that it can be seen from all over the village and the surrounding farm lands. On Sunday mornings, when the bells were ringing, the people from outlying houses would head towards the tower. It acted as a "beacon", which is why most churches have tall towers or spires.

In the village of Marbury there are some very old and some newer houses. Can you tell which are which? The village green, on the right, has an old oak tree growing in the middle, with a circular bench built around its trunk.

Q: The village inn is close to the green. What is it called?

A: "The Swan Inn".

16. **Continue along Wirswall Road, past old black and white houses.**

☺ On the left are some very old, wooden-framed buildings. The wood used for house frames was often oak, because it is strong and long-lasting. You can see it clearly, painted black. The parts in between the wooden frame are bricks, painted white. These houses are three or four hundred years old. Opposite them are some more black and white buildings, but if you look carefully you will see that these have no wooden frame, they are just brick which has been painted to look the same as the older houses over the road.

17. Pass the modern bungalows, then take the footpath on the left. Bear diagonally right to a further stile, then bear diagonally left.

The village inn, Marbury

☺ The church and lake soon come into view, and keep a look out for that transmitter you passed earlier on.

18. Take the stile straight ahead, then, in close succession, further stiles and a wooden footbridge over a small stream, lined with trees.

19. Avoid the stile to the immediate left, and continue straight ahead alongside a drainage ditch. At the far end of the field, take the stile almost hidden in the hedgerow. Bear diagonally right across the field.

☺ You should be able to see a large farm ahead. It has a metal haybarn in which bales of hay are stored to keep them dry.

20. Bear left along the lane, leading slightly uphill. Look out for the footpath in the trees on the right.

21. Follow the footpath straight ahead to a stile at the edge of the woods. Cross the stream via the plank bridge, and follow the path through the outskirts of the woods.

☺ If you keep quiet you may be able to see some rabbits or squirrels. There are rabbit holes close to the path, and there are sure to be squirrels around in the the trees. If they heard you coming, they may stay hidden.

22. Cross the stile at the end of the trees and cut across the field, bearing slightly to the right, to a stile in the hedgerow. Bear left along the lane to the canal bridge.

☺ Back to the canal now, and just a mile to go.

23. Cross the bridge and, immediately after, bear left to the towpath. Bear right and follow the path along the canal.

☺ On the other side of the canal there are open fields, probably with cows grazing on the grass. The transmitter looks a very long way away now.

There are many plants along the side of the canal, including thistles, nettles and reeds, which you saw earlier. There are also willow trees which have long, trailing branches. They like to grow close to water, in moist soil. Their bendy branches were once used for making baskets. Can you spot any willows?.

24. After some way the path passes under a bridge. Immediately after, bear right, uphill, back to the road and car park.

Big Mere and Marbury checklist

☐ A CANAL BOAT

☐ A DUCK

☐ A DUCK'S FEATHER

☐ A FIR CONE

☐ A WHITE COTTAGE

☐ A TRACTOR

☐ A BLACK AND WHITE COW

☐ A HORSE

☐ A WALKER WITH A RUCKSACK

☐ A CHURCH TOWER

☐ A BLACK AND WHITE HOUSE

☐ A PERSON WITH A DOG

The Cloud, Congleton

Also known as Bosley Cloud. A small piece of National Trust land on the Cheshire/Staffordshire border. It rises dramatically from the Cheshire Plain, and is visible for miles on the northern side. One of the few heathlands in Cheshire.

Starting point:	From Congleton, follow the A54 (signed for Buxton) out of the town. After crossing over the canal, take the third right turning and follow the road uphill. Head straight across at the crossroads, and the starting point is half a mile on the right, where there is a small lay-by between two driveways (SJ907634). Take care not to block the driveways. There are other lay-bys further along the lane.
Distance:	Short route: Just under 2 miles Longer route: 4½ miles
Terrain:	Some uphill stretches, but nothing severe. Paths across open heathland and dense woods. Longer route includes farm trackways and some distance along lanes.
Maps:	OS Landranger 118
Public Toilets:	None
Refreshments:	None in the vicinity
Pushchairs:	Totally unsuitable

1. **From the lay-by, take the stony trackway to the right, signed as a footpath, leading uphill. Pass a shuttered cottage on the left, and continue along the track as it bears around to the left. Take the steps leading steeply uphill on the right, signed for Cloud Summit.**

2. **At the top of the steps, continue ahead along the well-worn pathway, towards the trig. post at the summit.**

☺ To the right there are views over the surrounding countryside. The tower on the far hills is a transmitter which beams radio waves across the country. Further to the right you should be able to see Bosley Reservoir.

The path crosses moorland, with bracken and heather growing on it. Bracken is the fern-like plant which is green in the Spring and Summer, but turns yellow or brown in the Autumn. Heather is dark green and grows close to the ground, where there is more protection from the strong winds.It has small flowers of white, pink or purple. There are bilberry bushes which also grow close to the ground. They have small, oval, green leaves and purple/black berries in the Autumn. Can you recognize these plants?

The sandy path climbs uphill between the heather. On the right is a cliff face and a steep drop to the fields below. Don't get too close to the edge, and remember that the wind here can be very strong!

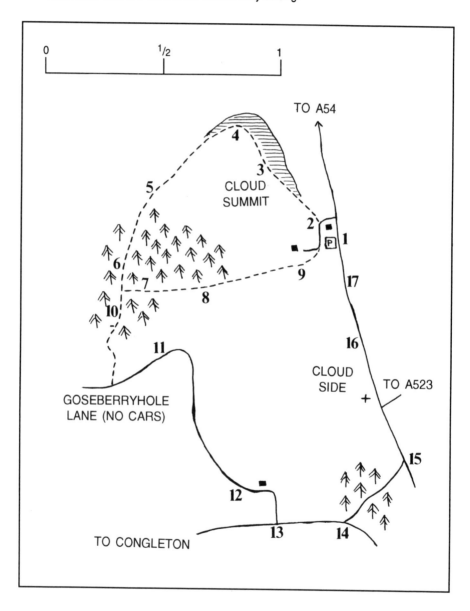

The highest point of a hill or mountain is called the "summit". At the summit here there is a white post (**ORDNANCE SURVEY TRIANGULATION POINT**) which proves that it is the highest point in the area, and the highest point in the walk.

3. **Continue straight past the trig. post, with the "cliff edge" on your right, towards the Cheshire Plain. It is a well-worn path.**

☺ There are views over the town of Congleton and a large sand quarry. Crossing over the valley below there is a long railway bridge with many arches. This is called a "viaduct".

4. **The path continues slightly downhill, bearing around to the left, towards the woods.**

☺ There are several young trees, mainly birch, growing out of heather and bilberry bushes. They take quite a battering from the wind.

5. **Follow the path as it skirts the woods for some way, before becoming engulfed by the trees.**

☺ Look for the dark, prickly gorse bushes which can have yellow flowers for most of the year. They make good shelters in which rabbits and hares can hide from passing walkers.

6. **Continue through the woods, looking for a "gateway" on the right, in the corner of the woods. Do not go through the gate. Instead, bear left, along a path running close to a dry-stone wall.**

(For the longer route go through the "gateway" and skip to direction 10)

7. **Follow the path through the trees, leading slightly uphill. Keep close to the dry-stone wall at all times.**

☺ The trees are mainly conifers which have tall straight trunks and needle-like leaves. Most conifers are evergreens; which means they do not lose their leaves in winter. Pine, fir and spruce are all types of evergreen conifers.

Trees that lose their leaves in the winter are called "deciduous". They are more common in this country than conifers. Sycamore, oak and birch are all deciduous trees. Can you tell which trees are conifers? Look for fir cones along the path.

Look for rabbits running away through the undergrowth of blackberries and bracken. There are many rabbit holes all over the woods. Can you see squirrels, in the treetops, or running up and down the trunks, looking for food? Over to the right there are views over the fields into Staffordshire. You may see people working on the land.

The view from The Cloud

8. At the top of the woods, take the stile in the right corner. Keep straight ahead across the field, with the drystone wall on the left.

🙂 Are there cows in this field? Black and white cows are the most common in this area. They are called "friesians" and eat grass by pulling it up with their rough tongues. Cows are very nosy and may approach you, but they are also very nervous, and are probably more afraid of you than you are of them. In the field over the wall there are often horses. Both cows and horses have long tails, which they flick in hot weather to ward off flies.

Q: You should pass a house on the left. How many chimney pots does it have?

A: Three.

9. Climb the makeshift stile on the left, at the end of the field. Bear right down the gravel driveway, leading downhill to the lay-by. This is the end of the shorter route.

10. Continuation of the longer route: From the woods, go through the gateway and follow the path as it leads away, between bracken and brambles. It winds downhill to a rough trackway called Goseberryhole Lane. Bear left.

🙂 The trackway is sandy, and possibly muddy in wet weather. Can you find any horses' hoofprints or the tyretracks of a tractor?

11. Follow the track as it bears to the right, leading slightly downhill.

🙂 To the left there are open fields and the woods of the Cloud. To the right there are views over the surrounding countryside of Staffordshire.

Along the track there are many fine old trees, including oaks and beech. There are also many hedgerow plants. Hogweed is a tall plant with a thick, stick-like stem and many clusters of white flowers. You may see some which are taller than you. Rosebay willow herb is also tall, it has pink flowers at the top of a thin stem.

12. Pass the farmhouse on the left and follow the track around to the right.

🙂 In the farm garden there are fruit trees, including damsons, apples and pears. In the Summer, you should be able to see the ripe fruit hanging from the branches.

13. Bear left along the lane. There are grass verges along most of this road.

🙂 If you look back to the left, you may be able to see the white stone at the summit of the Cloud, where you stood earlier in the walk.

Q: On the right is a house built of local sandstone. It has wooden shutters at the windows. How many chimneys does it have?

A: Two.

☺ Over on the left you should be able to see some large stones standing above the walls. These are called the"Bridestones" and were once part of a "burial chamber" which was like a large grave. It was built, several thousands of years ago, by one of the tribes of Stone Age people who lived in the area. The large stones form a sort of room, and over the top there would have been other stones, and possibly a mound of soil. The mound and many of the stones are now missing.

(To visit the Bridestones, bear left along the farm driveway and go through the gate on the left to the burial chamber. Return the same way to the lane and continue.)

Q: What is the name of the next house on the left?

A: The name of the house is on the gates. As it is so near to the old stones, it also is called "The Bridestones".

14.   Bear left along a narrow lane, cutting through trees.

Q: Notice the road sign. How far is it to Congleton?

A: 3¼ miles.

☺ Feeling tired? Less than a mile to go now . . .

15.   At the junction, bear left. Keep straight ahead. Avoid all other turnings.

☺ This is an area called Cloudside, because it is close to the Cloud.

Q: You should pass a farm on the right, named after a tree which you have seen many times today. What is the name of the farm?

A: "Beech Tree Farm".

☺ On the left, set back from the road, is a church. It doesn't have a tower or steeple, but you can tell which building it is because it has tall arched windows.

Q: Shortly, on the left, you will pass another house named after a tree. What is it called?

A: "Willow Cottage".

Q: On the left you will pass a house called "Lord's Acre". Do you know what an "acre" is?

A: It is a large measurement of land.

☺ Later there is another house called "Green Acres" and, on the right, look for the well in front of a house.

16.   Continue past a scrub field as the road begins to ascend slightly.

Q: Look for the triangular road sign at the top of the hill. It shows what looks like a "Y" upside down. Can you guess what it means?

A: It is a warning that the road gets narrower ahead.

17.   The lay-by/starting point is just ahead on the left.

The Cloud checklist

☐ A HORSE

☐ A RESERVOIR

☐ A SAND QUARRY

☐ HEATHER

☐ AN ACORN

☐ IVY

☐ A BLACK AND WHITE COW

☐ FUNGUS/TOADSTOOLS

☐ A STONE WALL

☐ A TRACTOR

☐ A WELL

☐ A DOG

𝕯elamere 𝓕orest

Delamere Forest was once part of a vast hunting ground, belonging to the Norman kings, which covered most of Cheshire. There are well-marked paths and trackways throughout the forest, and plenty of amenities for the family. It is still a working forest and areas may be closed for felling. Certain areas may have been felled, and others replanted, so allow a little leeway with the text. An ideal location for pushchairs, train travellers, naturalists and tea drinkers. If you fit into one or more of these categories, head straight for Delamere.

Starting point:	Delamere Forest Visitor Centre car park (SJ548704). Turn off the B5152 (Frodsham to Cotebrook road) at Delamere station and follow the driveway to the Visitor Centre. There are also other car parks along this drive.
By rail:	Delamere station, it couldn't be simpler. Trains from Chester and Manchester.
Distance:	6 miles
Terrain:	Good forest trackways and well-defined paths
Maps:	OS Landranger 117. Delamere Forest Visitors' Map, available from Visitor Centre
Public Toilets:	Visitor Centre. Barnbridge Gates car park
Refreshments:	Drinks machines at the Visitor Centre
	Delamere station: attractive cafe/tea-room in old station building with railway memorabilia on display. Other cafes and pubs in the area: at Hatchmere, Delamere village, Sandiway and Cotebrook.
Pushchairs:	An ideal route for pushchairs. For a very short circular route, park in the Barnsbridge Gates car park and follow the "Easitrail", specially designed for disabled people and pushchairs.

First call at the Visitor Centre, which has displays, exhibitions and information relating to the forest and the area. A gift shop, refreshments, toilets and cycle hire also here.

1. **From the Visitor Centre car park, bear right along the driveway, passing the Visitor Centre, then a house of painted brick on the right.**

Q: When was this house built?

A: 1906. There is a plaque bearing the date over the door.

2. **Continue along the trackway into the trees.**

☺ Many wild plants grow alongside the track, including blackberries, wild raspberries and nettles.

Q: If you are stung by a nettle, you can rub the sting with a certain leaf to stop it hurting. What type of leaf?

A: A dock leaf. They are quite large and oval, and can usually be found growing next to nettles. Can you see any?

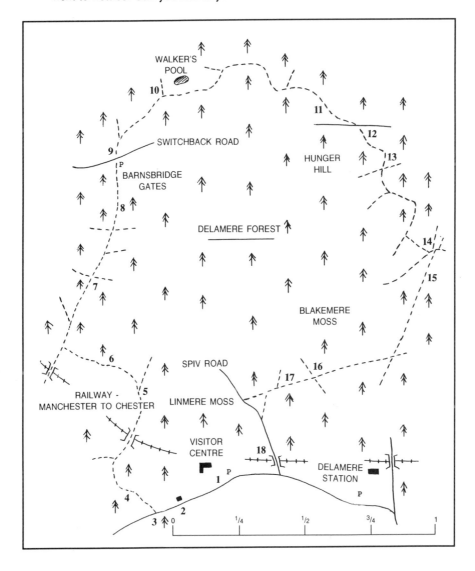

3. **Bear right along the first footpath (at post 13) into the forest.**

☺ This is an area of conifers which have dark green needles. They are grown, in this country, mainly for their wood. Pine is particularly popular for making furniture.

Amongst the other trees are occasional rowans which are easy to spot in the Summer or Autumn because of the bright orange or red berries.

4. **The path winds downhill between ferns and brambles. At the junction (at post 11) bear right and cross the bridge.**

☺ On the right, just before the bridge, is an area of beech trees. Can you recognise them? Beech trees can live for over 200 years, so these trees may have been here longer than the railway, that passes under the sandstone bridge, and most of the houses in the area.

Beeches, along with trees such as oak and sycamore, are called "broad leaved trees" because their leaves are wide and flat, unlike the needles of conifers. They are native to this country, which means they grow here naturally, unlike most conifers, which come from abroad and are planted here by man. Can you tell which trees are Conifers and which are Broad-leaved?

Q: After the bridge there are many Silver Birches on both sides of the path. They have narrow trunks with silver-white bark. Do you think they are Conifers or Broad-Leaved trees?

A: Broad-Leaved.

5. **Take the first left turning, along a wide gravel pathway, through conifers and mixed trees.**

☺ Different wood is used for making different things. A special willow is grown for making cricket bats. Sycamore is used for kitchenware, like cutting boards and wooden spoons. Horse chestnut is often used for making wooden toys. How many things can you name in your own home that are made of wood?

6. **Follow the path as it leads downhill through overhanging conifers to a junction (post 19), with a railway bridge off to the left. Bear right along a forest trackway. Keep right at the next junction.**

☺ On your walk through the forest you may come across areas that have been **FELLED**, or cleared of trees, and you will probably find stacks of logs waiting to be taken away. If you do, look at one of the round ends of the logs and count the rings. There should be a ring for each year. You will probably find the trees were twenty or thirty years old before they were felled.

You will also come across areas that have been newly planted with young trees.

These will be allowed to grow for many years, and will provide wood for the future.

7. **Go straight across at the crossroads (post 49) and continue ahead, keeping to the main trackway and avoiding all paths on either side.**

Escape Route: At the crossroads bear right. Keep to the main path which will lead you, in just over 1 mile, to a bridge over the railway. For the car park, bear right along the lane after the bridge.

☺ On both sides of the path there are some very tall conifers and sweet chestnut trees. These trees are very tall, but their roots will probably not go far down into the ground, (**USUALLY LESS THAN 8 FEET [2.5 METRES]**) but will spread over a very wide area, often as large as a football pitch.

Conifers are very fast growing, which is one reason why they are grown for wood. Sweet chestnuts are slower growing, but can live for over 400 years. That may seem like a long time, but the oldest trees in the world can be found in Canada and America, and are over *six thousand* years old.

8. **Keep to the main path, which leads to a road, take great care crossing over, and follow the sandy track through the forest opposite.**

(Just before the road, steps on the right lead down into the Barnsbridge Gates car park, where there are toilets and the start of the "Easitrail" for disabled people and pushchairs. There is also a notice board showing some of the many birds that frequent the forest.)

9. **Take the sandy trackway over the road which forms part of the Sandstone Trail. Bear right through conifers along the main path.**

☺ Through the trees on the left, you may see Walkers Pool, one of many small ponds within the forest. It is quite marshy in this area. The entire forest was once like this, but most of it has dried out.

Between the conifers on the left there are many silver birch. Their seeds grow very easily, and they can take over whole areas very quickly. There are also more rowans on both sides.

10. **Keep right.**

☺ All plants need light to live. Where the forest trees are growing very close together, no sunlight can reach the forest floor, so no plants can grow. Only dry, dead needles cover the ground. Here, the trees are not too close, and there are many ferns, blackberries and other plants growing beneath the trees. This jungle of greenery is called "undergrowth".

11. **Keep straight ahead at the crossroads, leading back to the road. Cross over and take the trackway opposite. (Passing post 30.)**

Forest trackway

There are many Broad-Leaved trees now: sweet chestnut, beech and rowan. Later there are mainly conifers.

12. **Keep to the main trackway, avoiding paths to either side.**

If you have a real Christmas tree, you may recognise it as a conifer. It is an ever-green, keeping its colour all year round. The needle-like leaves do not stay on the tree forever, they drop off slowly throughout the year and new leaves grow all the time, so the tree is never bare.

13. **Pass post 29 and keep to the main track, avoiding a path to the right. After a short way there is a wide, sandy path leading downhill, on the left (without a numbered post). Take this path, leading through overhanging conifers, to post 15 at the bottom.**

Acid rain is a problem which affects forests all over Europe. The fumes from cars and factories rise into the sky and mix with the clouds, so that when it rains the rainwater is acid. This damages the leaves of trees and whole forests have died. Thankfully, the problem does not affect Delamere Forest.

Pushchairs: In dry weather the rest of the route can be managed fairly easily. In wet weather, however, it is advisable to stick to the gravelled roadways. From post 15, bear right along the track, which will bear round to the left. Pass post

17, and at post 9, bear right for a short way. At the crossroads (post 10) bear left. Cross the railway bridge and bear right for the car park and Visitor Centre.

14. **Pass post 15 and continue straight ahead along the stony driveway, then bear right along a straight path of sand and soil between overhanging trees.**

☺ There are many animals and birds at Delamere. This is a quiet path, through the heart of the forest, and it is here that you are most likely to see the wildlife. Rabbits, squirrels, foxes and badgers live here, as well as cuckoos, swallows, owls and woodpeckers.

15. **Keep to the straight path, avoiding any small paths until you arrive at a broad crossroads, where there is a footpath post (unnumbered). Bear right along the wide, flat path.**

☺ There are still conifers on both sides of the path. Look for bilberries growing beneath the trees. They are low plants which have purple berries in the Summer and Autumn. These berries are not dangerous to eat, but you should never eat any wild fruit without asking an adult, as many may be poisonous.

16. **At the gravel trackway (post 5) go straight across and continue between banks of ferns.**

☺ Wild mushrooms and toadstools can be very poisonous. One type often grows under birch trees **(MANY ON EITHER SIDE OF THE PATH)** and has a bright red "cap" with white spots, so, if you see any, never touch them.

17. **Pass post 6 and continue straight ahead, passing a felled area on the right. Follow the path around to the left, and bear left along the gravel trackway.**

☺ From here there are views over the treetops towards the bare hills.

18. **Cross the railway bridge and bear right to the car park and Visitor Centre.**

Q: At the bridge there is a triangular sign with something like lightening on it. What do you think this means?

A: It is a warning that the wires ahead carry electricity and are very dangerous. You may see other road signs on your way home. Triangular ones like this are warnings, look for signs that mean old people crossing, roundabout ahead or sharp bends in the road.

Delamere Forest checklist

- [ ] A STONE BRIDGE
- [ ] BLACKBERRIES
- [ ] A COW
- [ ] A TRAIN
- [ ] A WHITE CAR
- [ ] A SQUIRREL
- [ ] A CONIFER/EVERGREEN TREE
- [ ] A SILVER BIRCH TREE
- [ ] SOMEONE WITH A DOG
- [ ] A CYCLE
- [ ] A PILE OF LOGS
- [ ] NEWLY PLANTED TREES

𝔇unham 𝔐assey and 𝔏ittle 𝔅ollington

Dunham Massey Hall was originally built in Tudor times, and was renowned as one of the finest halls in Cheshire. Since a reshuffling of the county boundary, it has been severed from Cheshire as the new boundary follows the course of the River Bollin around the edge of the parkland.

The Victorian novelist and biographer, Elizabeth Gaskell, referred to Dunham Massey as the "favourite resort of the Manchester workpeople". Today, little has changed in that respect. The hall, its gardens and parkland are now owned and preserved by the National Trust. Fallow deer roam throughout the park and the small pools attract a wealth of birdlife. The facilities in the stables provide a restaurant/cafe, gift shop, toilets and often free displays. The grounds are entirely flat and everything can be found in a relatively short space. Dunham Massey is,like Tatton or Lyme, ideally suited for families.

Starting point: Car park on the north of Charcoal Road (SJ746874) or Dunham Massey main car park (SJ732875). From the latter follow the paths to the hall, then begin at direction 5.

By bus: Services from Altrincham & Warrington, stops close to both starting points.

By rail: Nearest stations: Hale or Altrincham

Distance: Entire route: 3 miles

Terrain: Flat parkland, canal towpath, pavement through Dunham Town

Maps: OS Landranger 109

Public Toilets: The stables, Dunham Massey park. Including disabled toilets and baby changing facilities

Refreshments: Stables Restaurant, Dunham Massey

Pushchairs: The entire park is ideal for pushchairs, though all entrances, except via the main car park, have step stiles. With some degree of effort, the whole route can be managed with a pushchair, but some lifting over stiles will be necessary, and the narrower parts of the canal towpath require care.

---

1. **From the Charcoal Road car park, bear right along the road, crossing carefully to the gates of Dunham Massey park. Climb the step stile into the parkland, passing Charcoal Lodge on the left.**

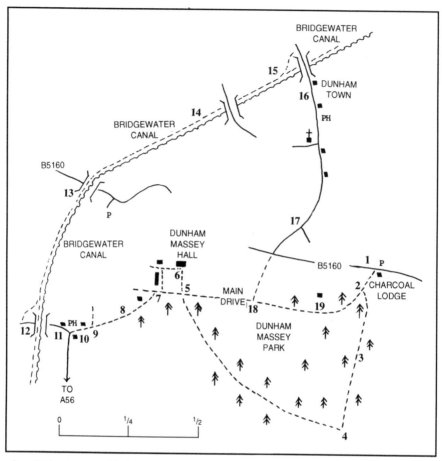

Q: This stone and brick house was the lodge, or gatehouse, of the hall in the park. What is the date on the plaque above the door?

A: 1906.

Just after the lodge there is a notice board with a useful plan of the parkland and hall.

2.   Immediately after the notice board, bear to the left along a wide, sandy pathway between ferns.

Escape Route: To make the route shorter, continue along the main drive, which will take you to the hall, then continue from direction 5.

Dunham Massey Hall

☺ On the left is the boundary wall, which marked the edge of the parkland belonging to the hall.

After a short way, notice the black and gold railings set in the wall. This allowed a good view from the hall, which you can see along the "avenue" of trees on your right.

Escape Route: To make the route slightly shorter, bear right here towards the hall and continue with direction 5.

3.   Continue along the sandy pathway.

☺ On the right is a Deer Sanctuary, a place where the deer can avoid people and raise their young. Deer are shy creatures. Do not approach them, or feed them, and do not go into the Sanctuary.

4.   Follow the path round to the right.

☺ The gate at the corner leads to "Home Farm", which at one time would have provided all the food for the lords of the manor and their servants.

Keep a look out for wild animals. Apart from the deer, you may see rabbits, foxes or even badgers. Badgers are **NOCTURNAL** which means they usually come out at night, but they can sometimes be seen after sunset. They live in long tunnels called **SETTS**. You can tell a badger sett from the hole of other animals because they usually have soil piled outside. The badgers have scraped this out with their strong paws.

(AT THE POND TOWARDS THE HALL.) The pond is surrounded by rushes and reeds, and in Summer is covered with water lilies. Here you may find coots (small black birds) and sometimes herons (which have long legs).

5. **Continue ahead towards the fountain in front of the hall.**

☺ There was once a castle where the house now stands, but little remains of this. The hall was rebuilt over 250 years ago, and was given to the National Trust in 1976 by the 10th Earl of Stamford, who was the last person to live here.

6. **At the fountain bear left towards the stable block, then left in front of the clock.**

Q: These were once stables, where the horses lived. On the roof there is a clocktower. What date is on the clock?

A: 1721.

In the stable block there are toilets, restaurant and National Trust gift shop. The lower stables are often open to walk through (free of charge) and still contain stalls where animals were kept.

☺ At each end of the stable block there are steps which ladies would climb to mount their horses. On the outside walls of the stables there are hooks and rings where the horses' reins could be tied.

7. **Continue ahead after the stables, and then bear right, passing the old mill on the right.**

☺ This building is Dunham Mill, where corn was ground to make bread for the whole estate. Through metal bars in the wall you can see a **(RESTORED)** waterwheel which would have turned the large stone wheels which ground the corn. Old millstones lean against the mill walls.

8. **Continue ahead over the step stile, and along the footpath between farmed fields.**

☺ The tall building ahead is Bollington Mill which is 150 years old. It has now been made into luxury flats. A small stream, choked with reeds and waterside plants, passes through an archway beneath the Mill.

9. **Keep ahead, passing Bollington Mill on the right. Continue across the narrow, metal footbridge to Little Bollington.**

☺ The river you have just crossed is the Bollin, from which the village of Little Bollington takes its name.

Q: What is the name of the first white house on the left after the bridge?
A: "The Mill House".

10. **Continue up the lane, passing "The Swan with Two Nicks" pub on the right.**

Q: What bird is painted on the sign of the pub ahead?
A: A swan.

There are seats outside the pub, and children are welcome.

11. **Bear right, passing a black and white thatched house on the corner. Follow the cobbled lane and pass under the bridge.**

☺ This bridge is called Bollington Under Bridge. It doesn't go under a road or railway, but a canal. If you hear water dripping under the bridge, don't worry. It will probably survive another few hundred years.

12. **Take the narrow path to the right, immediately after the bridge, which ascends to the canal. Bear left along the towpath.**

☺ This is the Bridgewater Canal. Canals are man-made, unlike rivers. Most canals were built to carry goods, such as coal or salt. Today roads are used instead, and the canals are used for pleasure boats.

On the right, over the fields, you should be able to see Dunham Massey Hall again.
This path along the canal is called a **TOWPATH** because at one time horses would walk along here, pulling or "towing" the canal boats. You may see thistles, nettles and blackberries growing close to the water.

13. **Continue along the canal, with the main Dunham road passing beneath you. The canal and towpath narrow here so take care!!!**

Escape Route: To return to the park, go down to the road and bear right. The main park gates are nearby on the right.

14. **Ahead is Dunham Town bridge. Go under the bridge and continue. After some way there are houses on the left.**

☺ You will probably see several houseboats along the canal. These are called **NARROW BOATS** because they are long and narrow. They are often painted in bright colours and decorated with flowers.

15. **Before the next bridge bear left alongside the metal fence, along a path which**

rises to road level. **Cross the bridge and continue along the lane. (Pavement on left.)**

☺ This is the village of Dunham Town. On the left is the village hall, built for local events. Next door is the old schoolhouse where the children of the village were taught. It is now someone's home. This road is named after the schoolhouse; School Lane.

Q: When was the schoolhouse built?

A: There is a plaque over the door showing the date. 1795.

Further along, also on the left, is the "Axe and Cleaver" pub, with tables outside.

The Church of Saint Mark's was built in 1864 – it has a small spire in the middle of the roof.

(On the left is Dunham Town Post Office and store.)

16. Continue along School Lane.

☺ Notice how many of the cottages along this lane are very similar and are painted in the same colour. These were once estate cottages, where the workers at the hall lived, or which could be rented from the Lord of the Manor. To save money, many villagers would grow vegetables in the small gardens, or on allotments nearby.

17. At the junction, bear right and cross the road to the park gate. Climb the step stile and follow the driveway.

☺ On the left is Smithy Pond where there are often ducks and water birds. Along the drive the National Trust have planted a new row of lime trees to form an attractive "avenue". Old paintings show there were once many avenues in the parkland, but many of the trees have died and not been replaced.

18. At the junction, bear left along the main drive.

☺ Here there is an avenue of oak trees. You may notice stumps where old trees have died or been cut down. New trees have been planted to replace them. Very young trees will be protected from the deer, as they like to eat the bark.

Q: What is a young tree called?

A: A sapling.

☺ Further along the drive, the trees forming the avenue are beeches. Could you tell the difference?

The building on the left, with arches around the outside, is the deerhouse. It was built over two hundred years ago and is still used today where the deer can shelter in bad weather.

19. **Follow the drive back to the lodge and cross the road to the car park.**

Dunham Massey checklist

☐ A DEER

☐ A STONE LION

☐ A CANAL BOAT

☐ A RABBIT

☐ AN OAK TREE

☐ A BLACK AND WHITE COW

☐ A FOUNTAIN

☐ A WATERWHEEL

☐ A BRICK BRIDGE

☐ A POST OFFICE

☐ A STONE WHEEL

☐ A DOG

𝓖reat 𝓑arrow

Great Barrow is a small village, a few miles east of Chester, in the midst of a rich, rural landscape, with many interesting and well-signed footpaths. There is a public house at each end of the walk.

Starting point: The church, Great Barrow (SJ470683). The village can be found on the B5132. If approached from the A51 there is parking on the left, opposite the houses.

By bus: Services from Chester. Bus stop on the main road.

Distance: 4½ miles, with various escape routes.

Maps: OS Landranger 117

Public Toilets: None

Refreshments: Pubs only

Pushchairs: Unsuitable

---

1.   From the main village street take one of the two unnamed lanes on the right which lead to the church. Climb the steps and bear to the right around the tower.

☺ This is the Church of Saint Bartholomew. The sandstone tower was added over 250 years ago.

Q: What shape is the stained/coloured glass window in the church tower?

A: Round.

2.   Bear right along the central path, between the graves, to the lych gate. Go through the gate and bear left along the grassy trackway.

☺ Look back at the tower. On the top is a flag pole, and a weathervane, which shows which way the wind is blowing.

3.   Just after the churchyard, bear left through a wooden gate and follow the footpath along a high wall. At the lane bear right.

☺ On an island in the middle of the road is an old water pump. At one time all the villagers collected their water from here. The stone trough that once caught the running water is now planted with flowers.

(On the wall, on the right, is a map of the village and surrounding countryside, with all the public footpaths clearly marked.)

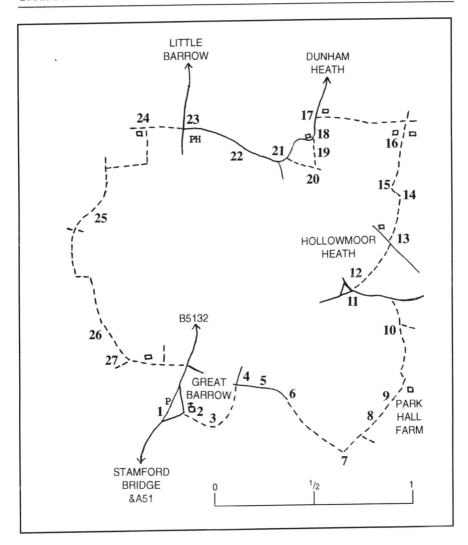

4. Continue down Mill Lane, which is signed as a dead end.

☺ The village is a mixture of old houses and quite modern ones. Can you tell which are old and which are newer? The newer houses are brick, while many of the older houses are stone.

Notice "Laundry Cottage" on the left. This may seem an unusual name, but it is quite common in old villages. Not surprisingly, laundry was once washed here.

Q: Can you find a house named after a prickly evergreen tree?

A: A brick house on the left – "Holly Cottage".

5. **Avoid the stile on the left. Continue ahead, over the stream to the end of the lane. The path continues just to the right of the gates to "Mill House". Keep left, avoiding the track bearing off to the right.**

☺ On the left is "Mill House", which gave the road its name (Mill Lane). It was once a mill, and in the garden you may be able to see the old weed-covered mill pond, and hear the sound of running water.

6. **After a short way, take the steps on the right, leading up the sandy bank and through a gate. Keep straight ahead along the edge of the field, with the hedge on your left.**

Q: Soon there are oak trees growing along the edge of the field. What is the "fruit" of the oak tree called?

A: An acorn. This is the seed of the oak tree, and if planted and watered it will grow into another tree. If you look back there are views of the church tower over the treetops.

7. **At the end of the field climb the stile and cross the plank bridge over the ditch. Bear left for a short way, then cross another plank bridge and stile. Continue ahead, signed for "Hollowmoor Heath". Soon a farm should come into view directly ahead.**

☺ As you can see, the fields are flat and surrounded by hedges. Many different plants make up a hedgerow. Can you recognise any of the plants in these hedges? Amongst them are hawthorns, with sharp thorns and colourful blossoms of white, pink or red in the Spring. Brambles or blackberries have prickly stems and also have white or pink flowers in the Spring. Their fruit is, of course, the blackberry. Another prickly plant in the hedgerow, which is quite common in this part of Cheshire, is the blackthorn or sloe, which has light green leaves and blackish berries in the Autumn. All these plants have "fruit" or berries which are eaten by birds and animals.

8. **Just before the farm take the stile on the left, next to a metal gate. Bear right and pass behind the farmhouse.**

☺ It may be muddy near the stile because there is a water trough nearby, and the cows come here to drink.

Q: How many chimney pots are there on the farmhouse?

A: Eight.

9. **At the corner of the field, veer left to the stile in the hedge, and bear left along the driveway.**

Q: What is the name of this farm?

A: "Park Hall Farm". There should be a metal sign near the gates, with horse-shoes on it. They are made of metal and stop the horse's hooves being worn away. Horseshoes are made by a "blacksmith" who makes things from iron. At one time it was a common job, but now it is quite rare. The horse-shoes are fitted onto the horse's hooves by a man called a "farrier".

10. **Ignore the footpath on the right near the houses. Follow the drive to the lane, then bear left. (There are grass verges along the lane.)**

☺ Over on the left you should be able to see the church again. There is holly in the hedges and more oak trees, which in Winter seem popular with large flocks of birds. Some birds "migrate" in the Winter, which means they fly south to other countries, where it is warmer. Others stay in Britain and brave the cold. They need a large amount of food to survive and would appreciate any nuts or bread crumbs you put out for them.

11. **Take the first road off to the right, but after a few paces take the stile on the right. Bear diagonally right, heading for the far corner of the field.**

Escape Route: Continue along the main lane which will bring you through the village and back to the water pump. Either follow the path back to the church, or bear right, passing the pub, to the main road and car park.

Alternatively, continue along the main lane for a short way, then take the footpath on the left. Follow this back to Mill Lane and bear right to the water pump. Return via the path to the church, or keep straight ahead, past the pub to the main road.

12. **Take the stile in the hedge, near the corner of the field and cross the plank bridge over a ditch. Continue ahead with the hedge on the right. Follow the path straight ahead and climb the stile onto the lane. Take the stile almost opposite, signed for "Manley" and follow the trackway.**

Q: There is a white house on the left. How many chimney pots does it have?

A: Four.

13. **Where the gates block the track, follow the fence to the left and climb the stile. Bear left along the edge of the field.**

☺ At this point, when I was walking the route, I heard a rustling noise in one of the trees. I thought it was probably a bird or a squirrel, but a fox scrambled from amongst the leaves and jumped to the ground. I was quite startled, and thought it might land on my head! It didn't! Once it was on the ground it ran into the hedgerow and disappeared. If you walk quietly and keep alert you never know what you'll see.

Foxes are related to dogs. Their coats are usually a reddish colour, though they are white underneath. They live to an average age of fourteen.

14. **At the end of the field climb the stile and bear left along the hedge. After a short way climb the stile to the right of the old metal gate. Cross the field, bearing diagonally right. The next stile is about half way along the field in the hedge opposite.**

☺ There are often cows in these fields and in Summer you may see them swishing their tails to keep off flies. Never walk close behind a cow or any large animal, in case you startle them and they kick out at you.

Near Great Barrow

15. **Climb the stile and cross the plank bridge. Head for the far right corner of the field, to a stile almost hidden in the hawthorn hedge. Cross this and continue straight ahead.**

☺ On the left there are hedges and undergrowth. Can you spot any hawthorn, with its sharp prickles and red berries in the Autumn and Winter? When all the leaves have fallen off, berries remain, which will be welcome food for small birds and animals during the Winter. Look for magpies, which are black and white birds, related to the crow. They like to build their nests high in hawthorn trees, so that they are protected by the sharp thorns. In the Autumn or Winter their nests can easily be seen. Magpies are often seen in pairs, and you may have heard the old rhyme: "one for sorrow, two for joy . . ." which is about magpies.

16. **Cross the next stile and go through the gate. Bear right, then left along the drive, with the house on your right. Go over the cattle grid and bear left along the stony trackway.**

☺ There are usually horses in the fields on the right. If a horse approaches with its ears forwards, it means it is interested, probably because it thinks you have food. If it has its ears back, it means it is frightened. You may see a horse rolling over on the grass. They do this to "groom" their coats. It helps to remove loose hair, and insects that may be crawling on them.

Q: What is the name of the white house on the right towards the end of the trackway?

A: "Hollingreen". There is a hanging sign with the name on it.

17. **Bear left along the lane, using the grass verges.**

☺ You may hear the sound of a train, as the railway between Chester and Manchester runs close by.

Are there horses in the fields on the left?

18. **Take the drive on the left after "Hollins Green Farm", signed as a public footpath.**

☺ The drive winds between hedgerows and leads to an old brick farmhouse. If you look at the stable doors you should see horseshoes.

19. **Go through the gates towards the house, and bear right over a cobbled area, and around the end of the building. Follow the grassy path downhill to the stile and continue ahead. Cross the wooden bridge over the stream and continue to the further stile.**

☺ On the left there are old, brick farm buildings and a rusting metal haybarn which will contain bales of hay in the Autumn and Winter. The hay is used for winter feed for cows and horses.

20. **Bear right along the driveway which winds back to the road. Bear left along the lane.**

Q: **(WHERE THE DRIVE JOINS THE LANE)** Opposite there is a house with stone animals guarding its gates. What are they?

A: Stone lions. Notice the unusual weather vane, in the shape of a tractor, on the garage roof.

21. At the junction bear right along Broomhill Lane, signed for "Little Barrow".

Q: How far is Little Barrow from here?

A: Look for the signpost to find out. Little Barrow is signed as being half a mile away.

Escape Route: Instead of turning off here, continue ahead along the lane and keep right for Great Barrow and the starting point.

22. Pass the houses on the left and continue along the lane.

☺ Further along the lane there are views to the right to the sandstone ridge that runs the length of the county. Along this ridge is a well-known long distance footpath called the Sandstone Trail.

Q: What is the name of the cottage on the right at the far end of the lane?

A: "Rose Cottage".

(On the opposite corner is "The Foxcote" pub which has a beer garden and children's play area)

23. Carefully cross the road and take the lane opposite the pub, signed for "Great Barrow" and other places.

Escape Route: In an emergency bear left and follow the road back to Great Barrow, 1 mile.

Q: How far is Great Barrow from here?

A: Again look at the signpost. Great Barrow is $1^1/2$ miles from here.

☺ The lane leads downhill. On both sides you should be able to see sandstone rock, which is made of millions of grains of sand. It can easily be cut and was often used for local buildings.

24. Look for the footpath on the left, directly before the brick bungalow. Climb the steps and continue straight ahead with the hedge on your right. After some way the hedge bears to the right. Stay with it and continue downhill. At the end of the field, climb the stile and bear left along the trackway.

☺ This old trackway runs between hedges and trees. These hedges have many different plants and trees. Can you recognise any of them? There is the familiar hawthorn, sloe or blackthorn, blackberries, nettles and oak trees. Keep a look out for rabbits and rabbit holes hidden in the sandy banks beneath the hedgerows.

25. Avoid footpaths on both sides and keep to the main track.

☺ You should soon pass an area of wild grasses along the path. Some of the grasses grow very high, perhaps taller than you. At the end of some of the stalks there are seeds which will eventually fall and, in the right conditions, will begin to grow.

There are occasional views between the hedges, on the right, over flat fields towards Chester.

26. **The track eventually bears round to the left. Avoid the path to the right and continue along the track, signed again for "Great Barrow ¼ mile".**

☺ On the left, in a garden, there are many holly trees, some of which have berries in the winter. Over on the right you may be able to see the church tower, which shows you that there isn't much further to go.

Q: What is the name of the black and white house which you should soon pass on the left?

A: It is called "Greysfield". It was built in 1878, and later enlarged.

27. **Follow the trackway to the lane, passing the school on the left. Bear right for the bus stop and parking lay-by.**

(Keep straight across for the 18th century "White Horse" pub, which is a short way on the right.)

Great Barrow checklist

☐ A HORSE

☐ A GRAVESTONE

☐ A TRACTOR

☐ AN ACORN

☐ A COW

☐ A HOLLY BUSH

☐ A WOODEN BRIDGE

☐ A BLACK & WHITE HOUSE

☐ A STONE LION

☐ A WHITE GATE

Great Budworth and Arley

Great Budworth is a delightful village, centred around the church and inn. It was featured, along with nearby Arley Hall, in Granada TV's quiz "Cluedo", when both places were visited by internationally famous stars. The countryside, despite its proximity to industrial Northwich and the constantly busy M6, is green, fertile and very attractive. A walk across the Arley Estate is rewarding in any season.

Starting point:	Great Budworth village (SJ664775) just off the A559. Well-signed from Northwich. Parking along the main village street.
By bus:	Services from Northwich and Warrington. Bus stop just outside the village on A559.
Distance:	6 miles – no escape routes
Terrain:	Mainly flat, footpaths across farmed fields. Some stretches along quiet lanes.
Maps:	OS Landrangers 109 and 118. Both maps are needed to cover entire route.
Public Toilets:	No public toilets along the route. Toilets at "George and Dragon", Great Budworth for patrons only. Nearest public toilets at Marbury Country Park, south-west of the village.
Refreshments:	Pub – "George and Dragon", Great Budworth. Tables outside. Children welcome. Popular at meal times, even throughout the week.
Pushchairs:	Unsuitable. Village and Lime walk only.

☺ This is the village of Great Budworth. It was once owned by the local squire (a rich landowner and country gentleman) to whom the villagers paid rent. This village was owned by the squire who lived at nearby Arley Hall.

Can you find a picture of a dragon anywhere in the village? Here's a clue – the village pub is called the "George and Dragon". Opposite the pub is the church, made of local sandstone. Its tower can be seen from miles away. The oldest parts of the church are nearly 700 years old, but it has been "restored" or renewed over the years. To the right of the church gates are the old stocks, in which criminals would be imprisoned. You can see holes for the arms and head. Sometimes people would throw rotten fruit at the person in the stocks. They were in use until 1854.

1.   **Go down the narrow cobbled street, School Lane, which runs alongside the church.**

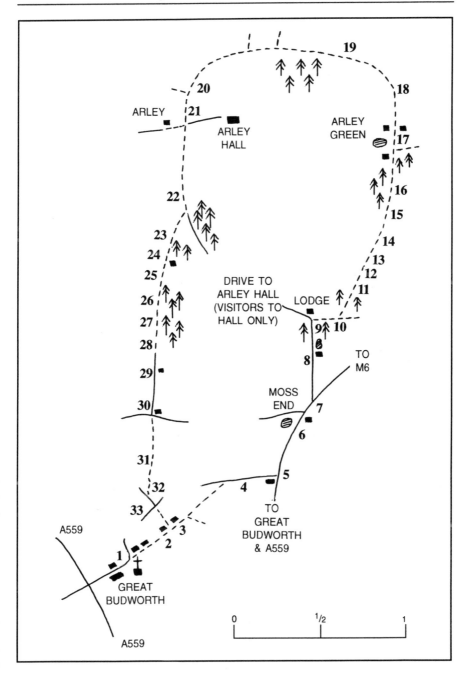

🙂 The cottages along the lane are very old, mainly made of brick with thick wooden frames, which you may be able to see. At the end of the lane is the village school.

2. After the school the lane bears around to the right, but on the bend there is a footpath leading straight ahead, between an avenue of lime trees. Follow the lime walk past the school field.

🙂 On the right there are views over the fields. In the distance you can probably see the smoking chimneys of Northwich, once a major salt mining town. There are several other salt mining areas in Cheshire, shown by place names ending in "wich". Middlewich and Nantwich are examples.

3. Avoid the stile and continue straight ahead. At the end of the avenue go through the gate and bear right along the lane. (There are grass verges for much of the way.)

🙂 Running close to the road are a series of pylons, carrying electric cables which you may hear crackling. The electrical voltage is very high, so it is very dangerous to climb a pylon. **(They do little to enhance the countryside either.)**

On the right there are more views over the countryside towards Northwich.

4. Continue along the lane towards the houses.

Q: After the modern houses there is an old thatched cottage on the corner. How many chimney pots are there on the main roof?
A: Four.

5. At the junction bear left, signed for Arley Hall. Again there are verges for most of the way.

🙂 As you pass under the wires hanging from the pylons, listen for the crackling which will be much louder in wet weather. Along the lane there are hawthorn hedges and wild plants such as blackberries and pink rosebay willow herb growing on the grassy banks. The hedges give shelter to birds and other small wild creatures.

6. Avoid the first junction and continue ahead.

🙂 On the left there is a small pond surrounded by reeds and bulrushes, with lilies on the surface of the water. This is the first of many ponds along the walk.

Q: What is the name of the house opposite the pond?
A: "Royal Oak Cottage".

7.   Pass a sign for Arley Hall, and take the next turning on the left.

Q: Look for a sign with a "T" on it. The top part of the "T" is red. What do you think this sign means?

A: It means that for cars this road is a dead-end; it doesn't go anywhere.

☺ "Arley Moss Farm" is over on the right. Can you see where a newer roof was added when the farmhouse was extended? Just after the farm there is another pond with ducks and geese, as well as bulrushes and a young weeping willow tree.

8.   Continue along the lane towards the entrance lodge of Arley Hall.

Q: The small building ahead is called "Willow Lodge". How many chimneys does it have?

A: Two.

(Anyone wishing to visit Arley Hall can shorten the walk by bearing left along the driveway, providing the hall is open. (Daily, except Monday, from April to October) At other times the driveway is private. After visiting the hall, return to the driveway and continue with direction 22.)

Arley Hall

9. **From "Willow Lodge", take the footpath off to the right, over a stile at the side of a five-barred gate.**

☺ Take care, as there are nettles along the path. You will probably recognise the large, oval leaves of docks which can be rubbed onto nettle stings to stop them hurting.

10. **After a short way there is a signpost pointing left. Follow the path to the left, as it leads through the trees to a stile. Continue straight ahead across the open field, passing the pond on your right.**

☺ There is another pond in the middle of the field and there will probably be an area of mud close to the water's edge where cows have gone to drink.

11. **There is a plank bridge over a ditch, then a stile. Continue straight across the field.**

☺ There may be cows in the fields. If the cows are lying down it supposedly means it is going to rain. It is certainly true that cows lie down when there is damp in the air, but it does not always mean that it will rain. Have you seen any cows lying down today? Do you think it is going to rain?

12. **Climb the stile to the left of the metal gate and continue straight across the field.**

☺ Manchester Airport is not very far from here, so you may see aeroplanes overhead as you cross the fields, and tractors ploughing or collecting crops.

13. **Again cross the bridge over the ditch and keep straight ahead.**

☺ There is another pond close to the stile, and woods on both sides in the distance. You can probably hear the sound of cars on the motorway, beyond the trees.

14. **Climb the stile and keep straight ahead, following the fence and row of oak trees.**

☺ These trees along the edge of the field are oaks. In the late Summer you should be able to see clusters of acorns at the ends of the branches. In the Autumn these will fall and some may start growing. They will not survive here because they will be ploughed up.

15. **After the next stile keep ahead, with the woods on your left.**

☺ This is a mixed wood with many different types of trees growing. Look for rabbit holes at the edge of the woods, and rabbits running for cover. You may see a flash of their white tails as they run away. This warns other rabbits that there is danger.

16. Continue towards the brick house and climb the stile to the left of the metal gate. Continue straight ahead along the drive, passing the house on the left. At the junction, a signpost indicates that there are several footpaths in all directions. Keep ahead towards the pond.

☺ Here is yet another pond. This one is quite large and has an island in the middle. Are there any ducks or geese on the water, or resting on the banks?

17. Continue along the drive, crossing Arley Brook and heading towards the buildings at Arley Green.

☺ After the pond there are houses on both sides of the path. On the left is an old black and white building which is built on sandstone blocks, which you can see at the bottom. This was once an old barn, but the squire from Arley Hall had it made into a school for his "tenants", the people who rented his cottages.

Q: The newer building next to it has many tall square chimneys. How many chimneys are there on the main roof?

A: Thirteen.

☺ On the right of the path there is an old water pump, and in a brick pillar behind is an old post box, from Queen Victoria's reign. It is probably over 100 years old. Victoria was the longest serving British monarch and was on the throne from 1837 to 1901.

18. Continue along the driveway.

☺ After a short way, you should be able to see Arley Hall over the fields on the left. The hall was the home of the squire and his family. It was built over 160 years ago. The bricks were made here, with clay dug locally. Parts of the hall were demolished nearly thirty years ago when they became unsafe and it would have been too expensive to repair them.

19. Avoid all footpaths and continue along the drive, which soon curves to the left.

☺ If you're tired, you're now half way around the walk, and the next half is easier.

20. The drive soon leads past farm buildings on the left and comes to a crossroads.

☺ (AT THE CROSSROADS) On the left there is a wooden sign which points back the way you have just come. On the sign there is a rhyme:

"No cartway save on sufferance, here
For horse and foot the road is clear
To Lymm High Legh Hoo Green & Mere"

This means that the road is not for vehicles, and should be used only by horses and people. The last line is a list of nearby places reached by the path. The rhyme was written by the squire who had the present hall built. His name was Rowland Egerton-Warburton, and he was known as "The Rhyming Poet of Arley".

Anyone wishing to visit the hall should bear left at the crossroads. It is a very attractive house with good grounds, but not recommended for young children.

21. Go straight across at the crossroads, pass the car parks and continue along the main driveway.

☺ In the parkland on the left are fine, old trees such as beech and oaks, and often cows grazing.

22. Take the footpath to the right some distance along the drive. Climb the stile and bear left along the edge of the field.

☺ These fields often grow crops such as wheat, corn or potatoes. If there is a crop in the field, see if you can tell what it is. Wheat is yellow and grass-like. At the end of the stalks there are small grains which are ground to make flour which is then used to make bread. The crops are collected or "harvested" in the late Summer or early Autumn. Much wheat is grown in Cheshire, and the county "coat of arms"/badge/symbol has three sheaves of wheat on it. A "sheaf" is a bundle, tied together in the middle. A common name for country pubs throughout the county is "The Wheat Sheaf".

23. Keep straight ahead. Cross the stile and continue alongside the plantation.

☺ Once the wheat is "harvested", short stalks are left sticking out of the ground. This is called "stubble" and the easiest way to remove it is to burn it. Afterwards the field will be ploughed ready for next year, or may be sown with grass seed.

In the trees, or running across the field, you may see several pheasants; colourful, nervous birds which tend to walk rather than fly, though they will fly if startled. They are bred in country areas.

24. Climb the next stile and continue straight ahead.

☺ You will pass a farm house and farm buildings on the left. There are often horses in the small fields near to the farmhouse.

25. Climb the stile, cross the farm driveway and continue along the footpath opposite.

☺ There may be cows or sheep in these fields. There are also many rabbits. Perhaps you can see some of their holes close to the hedge. Rabbits often dig their "burrows" under trees or hedges because the roots help to stop them collapsing.

26. Keep ahead, go through the gate at the end of the field and follow the winding path through the woods. Cross the stream by the second bridge.

☺ This is Arley Brook, the same stream that you passed earlier, near the pond. The water is very clear, and the bottom of the stream is sandy. There are plants hanging into the water which make shelter for small water creatures. Can you see any creatures in the water, like fish, snails or water beetles?

27. Follow the path to the left, climb the stile and keep to the left of the field, close to the hedge.

☺ Again, these fields are often used for food crops. Potatoes have thick green leaves and grow close to the soil. The actual potatoes do not grow on the plant like apples on a tree. They grow under the soil on the roots of the plant.

Corn grows very high. If there is corn in a field and it is fully grown, you will not be able to see over it.

28. Take the stile ahead and continue along the concrete driveway.

☺ The hedges on either side of the drive contain many wild plants, some have flowers or colourful berries, like hawthorn and rosehips. These hedges and the thick "undergrowth" provide food and shelter for animals, birds and insects. Do not step off the driveway as there is a ditch on each side which you may not be able to see because of all the plants.

In the distance you should be able to see the pylons that you passed earlier. There isn't much further to go now. (Just over a mile.)

29. Pass the house and continue along the drive.

Q: What is the name of the house on the left?
A: "Crabtree Cottage".

30. At the end of the drive, cross the lane and take the footpath opposite. Keep straight ahead, close to the fence on the right.

☺ Cows are often in these fields and you should pass a large water trough for their drinking water. Further along the field the church tower in the village of Great Budworth should come into view.

31. Climb the stile and bear left. Follow the edge of the field around to the right, leading slightly downhill, passing under the pylons.

☺ You should have a clear view over the village. There are some modern houses and many older ones, including some black and white cottages which have thatched roofs.

When you pass under the pylons you will probably hear the loud crackling of electricity.

32. **Climb the stile in the bottom corner of the field. Steps lead down to a narrow lane. Bear left.**

☺ Almost there now . . .

33. **At the junction head straight across, along a trackway, then bear right at the end, following the tree-lined footpath back to the village centre. Alternatively, bear right along the lane and follow the road around to the left which comes out facing the church.**

Other places of interest in the area

Marbury Country Park

South-west of Great Budworth. Pass through Comberbach and it is on the left. Further walks, bird-watching, picnic area, toilets. (For more information see Marbury Country Park route)

Pickmere

East of Great Budworth. Attractive lake, now a "water park" with boats for hire, windsurfing etc.

Great Budworth checklist

☐ A CHURCH TOWER

☐ A DRAGON

☐ A HORSE

☐ A TELEPHONE BOX

☐ A TRACTOR

☐ A POST BOX

☐ A BLACK AND WHITE COW

☐ A DUCK'S FEATHER

☐ A WATER PUMP

☐ AN OAK TREE

☐ A RHYME ON A WOODEN SIGN

☐ A PHEASANT

Little Budworth

Little Budworth is miles from its "Great" namesake, near Northwich, but both are picturesque villages with a church, an inn and a country park close by. Little Budworth common is several square miles of heathland with some very attractive countryside surrounding it. There are a wealth of footpaths in the area, but many of those crossing agricultural land are currently very badly signed with some poor stiles. This walk makes use of well-signed bridleways.

Starting point:	Little Budworth Common car park, on Coach Road (SJ591655). From Tarporley Road (A49) take the road opposite the Jardinerie Garden Centre. This is a long, straight road, and the car park can be found on the left towards the end. NB: Car park has a height barrier of 7' 6". Further parking is available just ahead, beneath the trees outside Oulton Park.
Distance:	3 miles
Terrain:	A relatively flat circuit across Little Budworth Common and sandy bridleways.
Maps:	OS Landranger 117
Public Toilets:	In the car park. Including disabled facilities.
Refreshments:	Pub in Little Budworth village. Cafe at Jardinerie Garden Centre at the top of Coach Road
Pushchairs:	The Common is flat and there are many wide paths between the trees, but most are soft and sandy, making it very difficult going for push-chairs.

1. **From the car park, turn left along Coach Road towards the gates of Oulton Park.**

☺ These are the ornamental gates of Oulton Park which is now well known as a racing track. At one time there was a large house on the site of the race track, and these were the East gates. The house burnt down in 1926. You may be able to hear the engines of racing cars. If you look through the gates you may be able to see cars going around the race track.

Q: What animal can you see on the coat of arms above the gates?
A: A red lion.

2. **From the gates, bear left, over an area of grass and beech trees, and then alongside the road into the village. (Pavements on both sides.)**

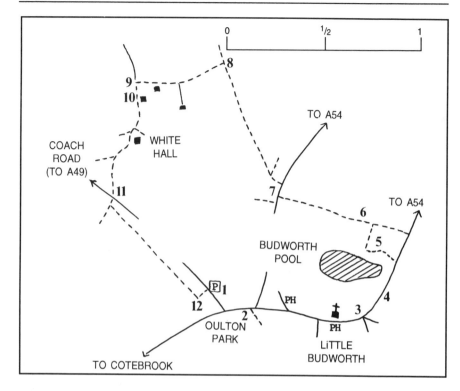

:) On the left is a tall cross which is a memorial to the men from the village who died in the First World War. Just behind the cross is a pub called the "Egerton Arms", named after the wealthy family that once lived at Oulton Park.

In the gardens on the left, can you spot a water pump which would have been used to pump water out of the ground, before running water was fitted.

Q: The village has a Church Room, which can be found on the right of this road. What is the date on the plaque on the front?

A: 1898

:) Next to the Church Room is the Old Vicarage, where the vicar would once have lived. It is made of whitewashed brick and has a thatched roof. Next to the telephone box is the Old Post Office. The new Post Office is now in the village store around the corner.

Q: What is the name of the cottage, with roses trained along its walls, to the left of the church?

Little Budworth

A: "Church Cottage".

☺ This is the Church of Saint Peter. The tower is made of sandstone and is the oldest part of the church. It was built in 1526, so it's very old. The rest of the church was built over 250 years later.

Q: What is the date around the clock on the church tower?
A: 1785.

Q: There is another pub in the village, opposite the church. What is it called?
A: "The Red Lion".

3.   **Follow the lane around to the left.**

Q: Here you can see the village post office. What initials can you see on the post box?
A: GR

4.   **The road winds downhill with pavement all the way. Avoid a track leading to a small mere and continue along the road, passing the edge of the water, then take the stile and follow the path through the undergrowth.**

☺ This is Budworth Pool, named after the village of Little Budworth. It has reeds and waterside plants around its edges. In summer there are colourful flowers which are popular with butterflies. There are often horses grazing in the fields next to the pool.

5.   **The path is often used and should be easy to follow. Take the stile to the right and through the field to a further stile onto a sandy trackway. Bear left.** There are views back over the pool to the church and village.

6.   **The track soon becomes enclosed by grassy banks and hedgerows, then opens out with fields on either side. Continue straight ahead to the lane.**

Escaperoute: Bear left along the lane then right, which will take you back to Oulton Park.

7.   **Bear right along the lane for a very short way, then take the trackway on the left between trees and hedges. Keep to the main trackway.**

☺ This track is used for horses. Can you see any hoof prints on the ground?

8.   **At the fork bear left. This leads to a tarmac farm driveway. Bear right along the drive, passing paddocks and stables on the left.**

☺ There are different types of trees on either side, including sycamore and oaks. There are several rowans which have red berries in the Summer and Autumn.

There are also holly bushes making up the hedges, and the houses on the left have been named after them: "Hollybush Bungalow" and "Hollybush Cottage".

9. **Bear left at the junction, passing two houses on the left. The lane then becomes a sandy trackway leading slightly downhill. Avoid the footpath to the left and keep to the main track, leading further downhill beneath overhanging trees. Keep left at the junction and cross a small stream.**

☺ Along the edges of the track there are blackberries and wild raspberries. Always ask an adult before eating wild fruit or berries as they may be poisonous. Look for fircones on the ground.

10. **Pass the house on the left, after which the path rises slightly. Pass "White Hall" on the left, then the drive becomes flat again and bears around to the left, into the trees of Little Budworth Common. Avoid all footpaths and continue along the drive.**

☺ This is Little Budworth Common, once part of an ancient hunting forest which covered most of the county of Cheshire. Today it is a **HEATH** because it is covered mainly with heather, though there are now many silver birch trees growing here. These reseed easily to make more trees. If you look around you will probably see a silver birch. They have slim, silvery-white trunks. Look for mushrooms and toadstools which can often be found on the ground where birch trees grow. Never eat any mushrooms or toadstools you find growing wild, as many types are deadly poisonous. If you like mushrooms, buy them from a greengrocer's!

11. **Cross the tarmac road and continue along the sandy path opposite. Take the first footpath to the left, which runs almost parallel with the road.**

☺ Here there are many silver birches, but also heather, which grows close to the ground and has small purple, pink or white flowers. There are also gorse bushes, which have dark, prickly leaves and yellow flowers.

The common is the home of many wild animals, including rabbits and hares. Rabbits live in **BURROWS** in the ground, but hares, which are larger, live mainly in the middle of thick bushes, like gorse. You may hear the sound of a woodpecker, chipping away at the trunk of a tree, looking for insects.

12. **Bear left and cross the road to the car park.**

Little Budworth checklist

☐ IVY ON A WALL
☐ A CHURCH TOWER
☐ A CLOCK
☐ A WHITE COTTAGE
☐ A STONE CROSS
☐ A DOG
☐ A HORSE
☐ A TRACTOR
☐ BLACKBERRIES
☐ A COW
☐ A RACING CAR
☐ A STREAM

Lyme Park

Lyme Park is set in the north-east corner of Cheshire and is part of the Peak District National Park. It is run by the National Trust and is a popular weekend venue for families and serious walkers alike. The park marks the start of many fine walks, including the Gritstone Trail, which runs for 18 miles and finishes in Staffordshire.

Lyme Hall was the home of the Legh family, who have lived within the park since the 1300s. The hall itself is open to the public (phone for current opening times – 01663 762023). The parkland is open daily from 8 until dusk. Entry to the park is free, but there is a parking charge for all but NT members. Other attractions include picnic areas, cafes, two breeds of deer and a children's adventure playground.

Starting point:	Route A: The main park gates, Disley (SJ966842)
	Route B: Main car park, Lyme Park (SJ962823). Climb the steps to the left of the National Trust office to the front of the hall and begin with direction 6.
By rail:	Nearest Station – Disley. Bear left along the main road to the park gates – half a mile.
By bus:	Frequent buses along A6 from Stockport and Buxton directions. Ask for Lyme Park, bus stops located close to main gates.
Distance:	Route A: Entire route, for users of public transport – 6 miles
	Route B: Shorter route for car drivers – 4 miles
Terrain:	Some uphill stretches on grassy moorland. Grassy paths, some gravelled.
Maps:	OS Landranger 109, OS Outdoor Leisure 1
Public Toilets:	Next to Park Coffee Shop, near mill pond. Also disabled toilets.
Refreshments:	Main car park, tea-room at hall, coffee shop near mill pond
Pushchairs:	Most of the main parkland is accessible for pushchairs but the moorland areas are not, making this route unsuitable. The park, however, has enough to entertain children for an entire day without having to stray far from the flat central parts.

1. **From the A6, walk along the driveway into Lyme, passing the main lodge on the right. Take care crossing the bridge over the railway and be on the lookout for traffic. Pass the entrance kiosk and continue along the flat grass, following the main drive.**

(There is a map here showing the park and surrounding moorland.)

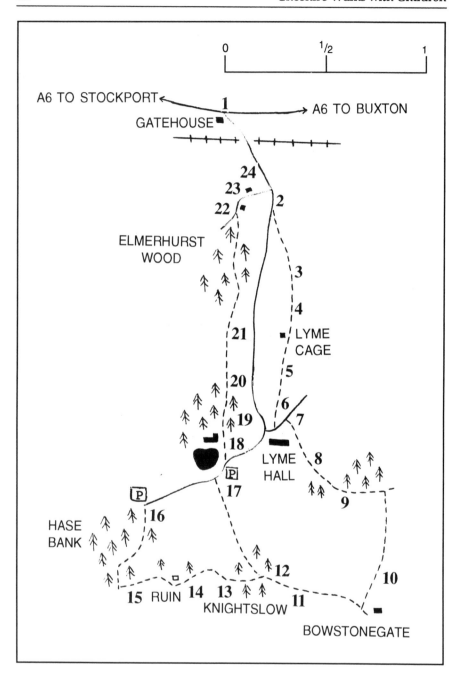

Lyme Hall from the Gardens

2. **The drive winds gently through attractive parkland. Look for a trackway leading off to the left. Follow this as it leads uphill between oak and sycamore trees.**

☺ Look for Lyme's famous deer which can often be seen in this area. They are shy and timid creatures, so do not go too near to them. The males have antlers. The females don't.

Q: What do you think deer eat?

A: Leaves, young shoots and occasionally nuts, fruit and bark.

☺ There are two types of deer in the park. Red deer are large and have a reddish brown coat. Fallow deer (like Bambi) are smaller and have white spots on their backs. If you spot any deer, see if you can tell which type they are.

3. **As you gain height, Lyme Cage comes into view.**

☺ Lyme Cage was built as a "viewing house" where the family from Lyme Hall could look out over the park and the surrounding countryside. It is supposedly haunted by a White Lady, who appeared every night to the shepherd and his family who once lived there.

4.   **Bear left along the track to the Cage.**

☺ You will notice that the windows in the Cage have been filled in because the building is old and unsafe. Some of the roof and inside walls were in danger of falling down.

From here, take a look at the views over Cheshire, Stockport and Manchester. Perhaps you can see where you live? There are two airports in sight, (Woodford and Manchester) so you may see 'planes taking off or landing.

Q: What are above the doors of the Cage and what are they used for?

A: Over each door there is a sun-dial which is used for telling the time...but only when the sun shines. On one side there is also an inscription; "Remember thou thy Creator in the days of thy youth".

5.   **Continue past the Cage on the main trackway. Where the path divides, take the right turning which leads gradually downhill. At the bottom it joins another trackway. Bear left along this to Lyme Hall.**

☺ This track was the main drive to the hall before the road was built. Horse drawn carriages would have driven along here, between the avenue of sycamore trees.

Lyme Hall is the largest house in Cheshire. The oldest parts are 400 years old, but most of it was rebuilt 200 years ago. The family who lived here had houses all over the north-west, and Lyme Hall was a sort of holiday home for them. In 1946 Richard Legh gave it to the National Trust.

The hall is supposedly haunted by the same White Lady who haunts the Cage. She has been sighted many times by visitors.

Q: What animals guard the top of the gateposts to the hall?
A: Stone lions.

6.   **Turn left in front of the hall and follow the road uphill.**

☺ There is another grand building to the right. This was the stable block where the horses were kept, and where the butler lived.

Q: What is on the top of the building above the archway and what is it for?
A: A weather vane, which shows which way the wind is blowing.

7.   **Go through the iron gate on the right, immediately after the stable block, and follow the stony trackway to another gate. Go through this into an open meadow. Continue along the track and climb the ladder stile at the end.**

☺ The tree next to the stile is a **LIME**, from which Lyme Park takes its name. These trees are all over the estate. (Limes (the fruit) don't grow on them.)

8. **Follow the path uphill into open moorland, keeping the wall close on the left.**

☺ **(ON THE RIGHT TOWARDS THE TOP OF THE HILL IS A DISUSED QUARRY.)** Gritstone was cut from this quarry. It is a particularly strong stone, and it is believed it was used in the building of the hall.

9. **Keep uphill alongside the wall. At the top bear right, continuing along the wall. Do not cross the stile.**

☺ **(AT THE STONE MONUMENT)** This is the highest point in the park and there are views all over the surrounding countryside: to the hall, the cage and all over Stockport. On top of the stone monument is a disc showing the distances of all the places you can see from here.

Q: How far is Stockport from here?

A: 6 miles.

10. **Continue along the wall, which now leads downhill. On the left are various aerials/masts and a whitewashed farmhouse at Bowstones. There is a stile on the left, but do not climb it, bear right, heading downhill on a well-worn pathway.**

☺ There are often herds of deer grazing on the moor and sometimes Highland Cattle with very long horns.

11. **At the bottom of the path climb the ladder stile into Knightslow Wood.**

Escape Route: To return to the car park, continue straight ahead along the main path which will take you back to the centre of the park.

12. **To continue with the route, bear left in Knightslow Wood and follow the path around the perimeter of the woods, keeping the wall on the left.**

☺ A ghost story...Look into the trees **(ON THE RIGHT)** and see if you can see anything moving among the shadows because these woods are supposed to be haunted...Long ago, one of the Lords of Lyme Hall was injured at war and was brought home to the hall, where he later died. According to the story, he was buried here, on the hill beneath the trees, and sometimes a ghostly funeral procession has been seen walking from the hall to these woods, carrying the body of the dead Knight. It is his daughter, Lady Blanche, who is said to haunt the hall and Cage.

Look for squirrels and fircones.

13. **Keep to the left, and you will come to a stile in the corner of the woods. Cross this and follow the steps downhill. Follow the path alongside the wall.**

☺ The land here is "eroding" or wearing away, partly because of the number of people who visit the park and use these footpaths. The National Trust, which owns the park, have to take care of the paths **(NOTICE HOW THE PATH IS SUPPORTED ON THE LEFT BY WOODEN PLANKS)** to make sure that they remain here for future generations.

On the right is a wall. It is called a "dry-stone" wall because no cement is used to hold it together. Many of these walls were built hundreds of years ago, but have survived because they were so well-made.

14. **Bear left, then climb the stony path through the trees to the ruin of Paddock Cottage.**

☺ This is the ruin of a small house called Paddock Cottage. It is several hundred years old, and was lived in by people who worked in the park until 60 years ago, when it became unsafe. Like the Cage on the hill, the windows and doors are blocked so people cannot enter.

From here there are good views over the moorland back to the white house at Bowstones, and over the Cheshire Plain.

15. **Continue past the ruin, heading towards the Cheshire Plain. Follow the grassy path leading downhill, with rhododendron bushes on the right. This soon becomes a stony and rutted trackway, winding down into Hase Bank Woods. Bear right along the driveway.**

☺ This was once one of the main drives to the hall. The many different types of tree here include conifers which are also called evergreens because most of them do not lose their leaves in the winter. Can you recognize them?.

16. **Go through the gate at the end of Hase Bank Woods, and follow the road to the right which leads back to the main car park.**

The low hill to the left of the drive is called The Knott. Anyone with surplus energy can climb to the top for further views over Stockport and over the park to Lyme Cage.

☺ There are often sheep grazing in this area. Can you can find any strands of wool on the grass?

In the main car park you will find refreshments and the National Trust Information Centre.

(Route B ends here)

17. **From the car park, take the road to the right of the millpond towards the toilets and Park Coffee Shop.**

☺ At one time these buildings were workshops. There was a waterwheel here which provided power for woodcutting. All the wood for the estate was cut here.

18. **Take the path to the right of the coffee shop and go through the gate into Crow Wood.**

☺ The houses on the left are called "Chestnut Cottages". In these woods are many Horse Chestnuts, from which conkers come. If it is late Summer or Autumn you may find some on the ground, but never try to knock them from the tree as this can damage it.

19. **Bear right over the stream, where there is a picnic table.**

☺ The water comes through a tunnel under the path. It is an overflow from the pond near the cafe. Along the banks of the stream there are ferns and reeds, and other moisture-loving plants.

20. **Continue along the path to the end of the woods. Climb the stile over the dry-stone wall and follow the steps uphill. Bear left along the path.**

(Down below, adjacent to the stream, are several sewage filtration beds, just in case anyone asks.)

☺ There are several beech trees along the path. In the Autumn you should see many beechnuts, which squirrels enjoy,on the ground.

Over to the right you should be able to see Lyme Cage on its hill.

21. **Follow the path down to a step stile into Elmerhurst Wood and follow the path.**

☺ This wood is of mixed trees, including willows along the stream. Further in the woods there is thick undergrowth, nettles and blackberries, as well as wild flowers. When the trees are very close together, no light can reach the ground, so no plants grow there. All plants need sunlight on their leaves to be able to grow. Where the trees are further apart, as here, plenty of sunshine can get through. On the ground you may see fallen trees which have started to rot. They make homes for thousands of insects which can easily burrow into the soft, decaying wood.

22. **Climb the ladder stile and bear right along the trackway.**

☺ You will pass "Northpark Cottages" on the right, which will have been built for park workers.

23. **Follow the track over two bridges, passing "Brookside Cottage" on the left.**

Q: On the left is "Brookside Cottage". How many chimney pots can you count on the main building?

A: There are four on the main house.

24.   **Continue to the main driveway and entrance kiosk. Bear left towards the park gates, again taking care at the narrow bridge. Watch out for oncoming vehicles.**

Lyme Park checklist

☐ A JOGGER

☐ A FIRCONE

☐ A DEER

☐ A PLANE IN FLIGHT

☐ A SHEEP

☐ A BLUE CAR

☐ A SQUIRREL

☐ A WHITE DUCK FEATHER

☐ A PERSON CYCLING

☐ A BLACK AND WHITE COW

☐ A PERSON WALKING THEIR DOG

☐ A RABBIT

𝓜𝓪𝓻𝓫𝓾𝓻𝔂 𝓬𝓸𝓾𝓷𝓽𝓻𝔂 𝓟𝓪𝓻𝓴

Marbury Country Park (near Northwich) was once the site of Marbury Hall, now demolished. It should not be confused with the village of Marbury, near Whitchurch. The grounds of the old hall are open to the public, and there are walks through woodlands, parkland and along the lake and canal. Just a stone's throw from industrial Northwich, but quite different.

Starting point:	The car park, Marbury Country Park (SJ652763). Go along the drive and take the first left turning into the car park. Marbury can be found between the A533 and A559 just outside Northwich, and is well-signed.
By bus:	Services from Northwich and Warrington. Stops close to the park entrance.
By rail:	Nearest station – Northwich 1½ miles away. Bus service available to complete the journey. From Lostock Gralam station it is possible to walk almost all the way along the canal (2 miles).
Distance:	2 miles.
Terrain:	Mainly flat paths, mostly gravelled, across parkland and through woods.
Maps:	OS Landranger 118
Public Toilets:	In the park. Disabled facilities also.
Refreshments:	None on site. Pubs at nearby villages of Comberbach and Great Budworth. Pubs, cafes & restaurants in Northwich.
Pushchairs:	The paths in the parkland are flat and gravelled. The route along the lake is bumpy in parts, but easily manageable. Avoid the last section through Hopyards Wood, and follow the pushchair route back to car park.

1. **From the car park, take the steps, passing the information board on the left, and bear left along the driveway to a further notice board.**

(Just ahead, to the left of the main pathway, there are toilets and an information room. On the left, in the trees, is a small picnic area.)

2. **Take the footpath on the left, just before the toilets, signed for the site of the old hall.**

☺ The park was once the grounds of a large house and this path passes the site of a previous rose garden.

3. **Continue to the site of the old hall.**

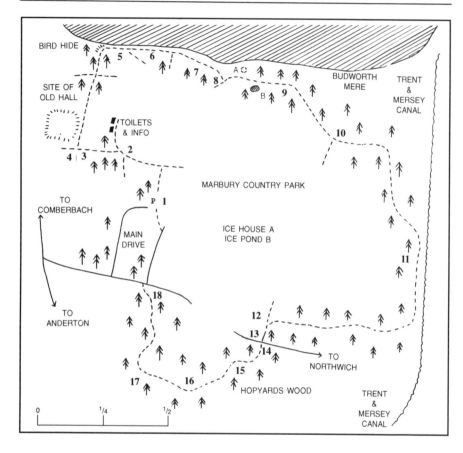

These low walls show where part of the old hall once stood. There is a notice board showing a plan of the house. It was built over 150 years ago as a family home...quite a large one! Later it was sold and became a club for rich country gentlemen. During the Second World War the house and grounds were used as a Prisoner of War camp, where foreign soldiers lived. In 1968 the house had to be demolished because it needed too many repairs. The hall survived for 126 years, which isn't very long for a large country house. Other halls in Cheshire are several hundreds of years old.

Just ahead is a figure of a woman, sculpted from an elm tree which was felled because it had Dutch Elm disease. Her name is "Elmer", which is a sort of joke.

The main driveway to the hall, along which horses and carriages, and later cars, would drive, went between the rows of trees.

4. Bear right at the house and go down the various flights of stone steps (or the grassy slopes if you have a pushchair) towards the lake. Straight ahead is a bird hide, overlooking the water.

☺ **(AT THE HIDE)** This is called a "hide". It is a place where you can sit and watch the birds on the lake, without them being able to see you. If you look through the slits you should be able to see the lake and the reeds along the opposite banks. There are many different types of water bird that visit the lake, including mallards, herons, coots and swans. How many can you spot? There is a chart showing pictures of the birds, to help you recognize them.

Someone who is interested in birds and bird-watching is called an "ornithologist". Are you an ornithologist?

5. Continue along the lakeside path.

(Pushchairs:bear right up the slope which leads through the trees to an open field. Take the second left turning, passing the avenue of lime trees and several wooden benches. Take the next left to return to the lakeside, and bear right at the water.)

6. Continue along the lakeside path, passing behind the boathouse.

Budworth Mere from Marbury Country Park

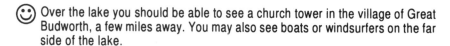 Over the lake you should be able to see a church tower in the village of Great Budworth, a few miles away. You may also see boats or windsurfers on the far side of the lake.

Along the edges of the water there may be a green floating weed, called "algae", which is eaten by fish and other animals. Close to the water, in fact, growing in it, there are several willow trees which grow well in damp places. They are often found in similar situations.

No swimming is allowed in the lake. It is reserved for ducks and birds, and they would be disturbed if there were people splashing about. There is also weed growing under the water which could wrap around a person's legs. Water is very dangerous, so never play near to it without an adult.

You may notice that in some places the bank has begun to collapse into the lake. New reeds and water plants have been planted to try and stop this happening in the future. The roots of these plants will help to retain the soil.

On the right of the path there is a sandy bank. Can you find any rabbit holes? There are certainly many rabbits living in the woods. Perhaps if you are quiet and look carefully you will see one.

7.   **Continue ahead along the lakeshore path.**

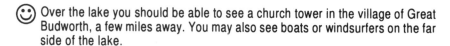 You should soon come across a telescope which looks out over the lake. Looking through a telescope or binoculars makes something seem nearer than it is, so you could look at things on the other side of the lake and see them clearly.

8.   **After the telescope follow the path uphill and bear left, signed for the canal via Big Wood**

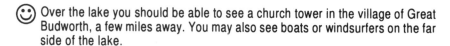 In the trees on the left is a circular hole surrounded by brick. This was once the entrance to an ice house, which was a room underground where blocks of ice could be stored throughout the year. The ice would have been used at the hall for keeping food cold and fresh, and in drinks, of course, It is colder underground and there would be no sunlight to warm it up, so even in hot, sunny weather the ice would not melt.

Over on the right of the path is the ice pond, where blocks of ice were cut in the winter to be moved to the ice house. Small chunks of ice would be taken to the hall when they were needed. A freezer is less trouble, isn't it?

9.   **Avoid minor paths off in each direction. Follow the main path which soon leads downhill to a wooden bridge crossing a drainage ditch. After the bridge, continue along the path as it leads uphill (and is somewhat bumpy), moving away from the mere.**

Escape Route: At the junction bear right, signed for Hopyards Wood. Take the second path on the right, between open fields, and continue to the car park.

10. **At the junction bear left. Keep to the main path which soon bears around to the right. Cross the wooden footbridge and continue along the main gravel pathway to the canal.**

☺ This is the Trent and Mersey Canal which was built in 1777 to transport goods from Stoke on Trent, home of the pottery industry. Soon the Cheshire salt mines were also using the canal to carry their salt. The nearby town of Northwich is well known as a salt mining town.

11. **Follow the path as it runs parallel to the canal for a short way, then bears away into the trees.**

☺ Before the path leaves the canal, look for canal boats. They no longer carry salt or pottery, which are transported by road or rail. The canals are used mainly for pleasure, for boating holidays.

12. **At the junction bear left, signed for Hopyards Wood.**

EscapeRoute/PushchairRoute:At the junction bear right, then take the first path on the left, between open fields, which will take you back to the car park/toilets etc.

13. **Carefully cross the driveway and enter the woods opposite. Follow the path as it leads slightly downhill.**

☺ There are many different trees in the woods, including sycamores. Can you recognize them? They are common in towns and can be found in parks or peoples' gardens. In the Autumn they have seeds in "keys" or "helicopters" which blow away with the wind. If it is Autumn, you will probably see them on the ground.

14. **Follow the steps leading downhill, then bear right over the plank bridge, after which the path runs close to the stream for some way.**

☺ This stream, Cogshall Brook, has sandy banks, as the soil here, and in most of Cheshire, is very sandy. Along the brook there are nettles and blackberry bushes, and many trees with overhanging branches.

15. **Cross a series of small bridges and a set of wooden stepping "stones" over ditches and muddy areas.**

☺ The "keys" or "helicopters" contain the seeds of the sycamore tree. All trees have seeds which can grow into new trees. There are several elderberry trees in the woods. See if you can spot any. They have clusters of green berries in the Summer, which ripen and turn purple or black in the Autumn. The seeds are inside the berries. There are also oak trees in the woods. The seed of the oak tree is an acorn, which you have probably seen many times. See if you can find any acorns on the ground.

16. The path winds slightly away from the stream and there are further bridges.

17. Look for the signpost pointing to the right and follow the path uphill. It winds to the left, then a set of steps lead up to the driveway.

☺ Ivy thrives nearby. It can cover large areas of the ground and grow up the trunks of trees. It has tiny suckers so that it can attach itself to the bark. Ivy is an "evergreen" plant, which means that it does not lose its leaves in the Autumn, but stays green all year.

18. Cross the driveway and take the trackway opposite. After a short way, bear left through the barbecue and picnic area and continue to the car park.

Marbury Country Park checklist

☐ A BLACK AND WHITE COW

☐ A CANAL BOAT

☐ A SWAN

☐ A CHURCH TOWER

☐ A PERSON WITH A DOG

☐ A WOODEN STATUE

☐ A DUCK

☐ A SQUIRREL

☐ A HOLLY BUSH

☐ A WHITE CAR

☐ A WOODEN FOOTBRIDGE

☐ A HORSE

Over Peover

Not to be confused with its sister village, Lower Peover, which is a couple of miles to the west. Over Peover, also known as Peover Superior, is a flat and attractive rural area, overlooked by the Jodrell Bank telescope, and, as a bonus, it has a selection of fine inns on its doorstep. Peover, incidentally, is pronounced "peever" and is Anglo-Saxon, meaning "bright river", after the small river, the Peover Eye, that runs close by.

Starting point:	Stocks Lane, Over Peover (SJ780741), close to the sharp bend in the road, where there is an old signpost pointing to, amongst other places, Peover Hall. Room for careful parking along the sides of Stocks Lane.
	Over Peover can be reached from the A50 Knutsford to Holmes Chapel road. Turn off at the Whipping Stocks inn, signed for Radbroke Hall & Stocks Lane. One mile along the lane there is space for parking, just before the road bears round to the left.
By bus:	Services to Over Peover from Macclesfield, Knutsford and Northwich.
Distance:	Entire route – 6 miles Shorter route – 4 miles Plus various escape routes
Terrain:	Flat footpaths or trackways for most of the way. The woodland along the Peover Eye stretch will probably be muddy in wet weather and can easily be avoided using the escape route.
Maps:	OS Landranger 118.
Public Toilets:	Toilets at "The Whipping Stocks" inn for patrons only. No public toilets.
Refreshments:	"The Whipping Stocks", Stocks Lane.
Pushchairs:	Unsuitable for pushchairs

1. **From the sharp bend in the road, follow the narrow driveway signed as a footpath to Peover Hall, passing a row of small brick cottages on the left.**

   ☺ One of these cottages was, until recently, the village Post Office. Can you guess which? It was the one with the post box in the wall next to its front door. In the garden, close to the door, there is an old water pump which was used to pump water out of the ground before running water was fitted. It is no longer in use. Imagine having to go outside on a cold, winter's day, every time you wanted water.

2. **Pass the long wooden building (which is the village hall) and continue along the drive, going through the white gates onto the Peover Hall estate.**

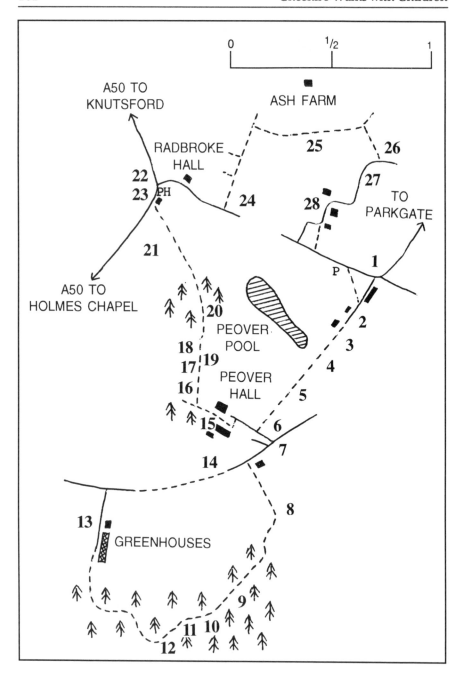

☺ **(AT THE HOUSE ON THE RIGHT)** This is "Peover Cottage". It is built of brick, and has a roof of stone slabs. Over the door there is a "coat of arms" which all rich families had to show that something belonged to them. This coat of arms is quite worn and difficult to see, but it has a shield and two helmets from suits of armour on it.

3. **Continue along the drive, passing the stables on the right and avoid all turnings off the driveway. Keep straight ahead, through a gate, along a fenced avenue of lime trees.**

☺ These rows of trees have been planted to form an attractive walkway which leads to Peover Hall. On either side are fields, and you may see sheep, cows or horses grazing.

4. **At the end of the avenue climb the stile and cross the footbridge.**

☺ This is Peover Pool. Along the edges of the pool there are many reeds and thistles and, in Spring and Summer, you will see lilies floating. The flowers close at night and only become fully open by about midday, or not at all if the weather is bad. In Spring you may see "frogspawn" in the reeds around the edge of the pond. Frogspawn is hundreds of frogs' eggs which are kept safe in a clear jelly. The female frog lays about 3000 eggs in March, and it takes two or three weeks for them to hatch, depending on how warm the weather is.

Q: Do you know what the spawn is called when it hatches?

A: It is a tadpole. When it first hatches it has a tail, but no legs. As it grows bigger, legs begin to grow until it becomes a frog, and can live on land, as well as in water.

5. **Continue straight ahead across the parkland.**

☺ Look **(TO THE LEFT)** for the huge dish of the Jodrell Bank Radio Telescope, towering above the tree tops. The dish is directed into the sky and can pick up signals from space. It has been used to track many of the rockets that have been launched from America.

Look for Peover Hall, which should come into view between the trees. **(AHEAD AND TO THE RIGHT)** The hall was built by Sir Ralph Mainwaring in 1585, over 400 years ago. His family lived there for many years. The last Lady Mainwaring gave all her servants red jackets for Christmas so that she could see them easily and make sure they were hard at work. Today, the hall is owned by another family.

6. **Climb the stile at the opposite end of the field which will bring you onto the main drive, close to the ornamental gates of the hall. Turn left, heading away from the hall, along the driveway which passes beneath overhanging trees.**

Peover Hall

Escape Route: To avoid the woods in bad weather, or to make the route 2 miles shorter, bear right at the stile, to the stables and coach house, (not through the ornamental gates.) Continue from direction 15.

7.   At the junction bear right along the main roadway, avoiding the right turning signed "to the church". Keep straight ahead, passing a farm driveway on the left. Just after the farm, take the stile on the left and continue towards the woods, keeping the wire fence on your left.

Q: There are often horses in these fields. Do you know what a female horse is called?

A: A female horse is called a mare. A male is called a stallion.

8.   At the bottom of the field bear right, and follow the edge of the woods for a short way until you come across a gateway and a footpath signpost, pointing into the woods. Follow the path downhill between the trees.

☺ These are mixed woods with many different types of trees including oak, sycamore, horse chestnut, and rhododendron bushes which have dark green leaves all the year round. Through the summer months they have large, colourful flowers of red, white, pink or lilac.

Q: What colour is lilac?

A: A sort of pale purple. Most wild rhododendrons are this colour.

9. Follow the path between ferns and brambles to the river, the Peover Eye, and bear right. If the path becomes hard to follow, look for white paint dots on the trees, which indicate the way.

☺ Notice the sand at the bottom of the stream. Millions of years ago, long before there were people, much more of the planet was covered in water than it is today, and the Cheshire Plain was at the bottom of the sea. This is why there is so much sand in the county.

10. Do not cross at the footbridge. Continue along the path, which keeps fairly close to the river for some way. Remember to follow the white dots.

☺ These woods are very dark and mysterious, and very quiet. Unless it is the busiest time of the weekend you may not see anyone at all, but there are eyes watching you.....look out for rabbits hiding in the undergrowth, keeping still, waiting until you pass before they move, and squirrels running along the branches above you, or disappearing up the trunks of the tall trees. There are many insects as well. Look out for spiders hanging from webs in front of you, and try not to walk into them. **(AS I DID!)**

11. The path undulates for a while, but still keeps fairly close to the river.

☺ Conkers come from horse chestnut trees, but you will only find them in the Autumn. Only pick them off the ground, never try to knock them from the trees as this can damage the tree and you may be in trouble if you are caught!

12. As an open field comes into view on the opposite bank, the path bears away from the river, leading uphill through ferns and brambles. Look for the white dots. Follow the path down into a gully, cross the footbridge and continue uphill to the gate. Go through the gate and bear right, along the edge of the field, towards the greenhouses.

☺ **(AT THE GREENHOUSE)** Glasshouses or 'greenhouses' are used for growing plants that need warmth, and could not survive outside. What can you see growing inside? There may be young tomato plants, and almost certainly colourful flowers like chrysanthemums. If you ever buy flowers, it is likely that they were grown in a greenhouse, like this. Sometimes you can see people inside cutting the flowers to put into bunches to sell.

13. Pass the farmhouse and continue along the lane, passing further greenhouses. At the junction, bear right along the gravel track. Soon it is surrounded by woodland and becomes a cobbled pathway. Keep straight ahead.

Q: What are the names of the brick houses you will pass on the left?

A: "Saint Anthony's".

14.   **Pass the footpath on the right and return along the driveway to the ornamen-tal gates. Continue ahead to the left of the gates, in front of the old stable block. Do not go through the gates to the hall.**

Q: This was once a stable block, where the horses lived. Lady Mainwaring of Peover Hall had it built for her son, Thomas. In which year?

A: 1654. There is a plaque over the door with an inscription and date.

Next to the stables is a similar building which is the Coach House, where carriages would be kept. It was built over 100 years after the stables. On the front of the building there is a clock and on the roof there is a small belltower.

Q: Find a set of steps which don't lead anywhere. Can you guess what they were for?

A: Ladies would climb the steps to mount their horses.

15.   **After the coach house turn left through the white gates, then bear right alongside the brick garden wall.**

(The gate into the gardens is on the right. The gardens are open to the public on Monday and Thursday afternoons. Payment is by an honesty box.)

☺ On the right is a strange piece of square stone with lines and numbers on it. It is a sundial and can be used to tell the time, but only when the sun shines. The metal bar casts a shadow on the numbers. It is like the hand of a clock. See if you can tell the time by it.

Towards the end of the drive you may notice several small gravestones. This is the pets' graveyard, where the owners of the hall buried their animal companions.

16.   **Take the paved pathway to the right, directly before the sundial, passing through the trees to the Church of Saint Lawrence.**

☺ The oldest parts of the church are 550 years old, but most of it was rebuilt nearly 200 years ago. In the graveyard, close to the bench, there is a large yew tree. Yews have dark green, needle-like leaves which they do not lose in the winter. Yews can live for thousands of years.

17.   **From the church, go along the tree-lined walk which runs past the graveyard. This opens onto a gravel pathway through the gardens. Keep straight ahead.**

☺ There is a tall wall on the left. On the other side is the Kitchen Garden, where all the fruit and vegetables were grown for the Lord of the Manor and his family. The huts along the wall will have been for the gardeners' tools, and the men probably had five minutes rest, safely out of sight of Lady Mainwaring.

18. **Continue ahead, following the arrow on the footpath sign. Pass by the steps on the left and keep to the main path as the grounds on either side are private. Continue through the trees and climb the stile. Bear left to a further stile and keep right along the edge of the field.**

☺ The long brick wall **(ON THE RIGHT)** separates the gardens of the hall from the parkland. You may be able to see a gold ball above the wall which is part of the roof of a summerhouse, where the lord of the manor could sit with his family on warm, Summer days.

During the Second World War the hall was used as a headquarters for the American Army. Hundreds of soldiers lived in huts in the grounds around you.

19. **Keep to the edge of the field and take the stile in the fence. Bear left along the stony driveway.**

☺ There are good views back over the parkland to the hall and church.

You will soon come to the other end of Peover Pool. There are reeds and rushes along its banks, and weed on the surface. Perhaps there are some ducks or coots.

20. **Cross the bridge and continue along the driveway.**

☺ Look for another pond **(ON THE RIGHT TOWARDS THE END OF THE TREES)**. It is only small and is covered by floating "blanket weed" which tiny creatures, like water beetles and snails, can eat. The more plants there are in and around a pond, the more wild creatures will live there, as the plants provide food, shelter and protection. Even in the Winter there is plenty of life under the water. A small pond like this will easily freeze over, and the layer of ice, rather than making the water cold, maintains the temperature. In the Autumn dead leaves will fall into the pond and will eventually sink to the bottom, making warm layers for the underwater creatures to live in throughout the winter.

Soon after the pond there are more horse chestnut trees forming an "avenue" along the driveway. They have wooden fences around them to protect them from cows and other animals.

21. **Continue through the white gates, passing the entrance lodge on the right.**

☺ This is "Peover Lodge" which was built nearly 200 years ago. You may notice that tree trunks were used to make the corners of the house. It has unusual arched windows, and colourful hanging baskets. There are small monkey puzzle trees in pots around the Lodge. They have dark, prickly leaves and supposedly get their name because monkeys cannot puzzle out how to climb them.

22. Bear right, passing "The Whipping Stocks" pub.

(There is a beer garden and children are welcome.)

☺ The hanging sign outside the inn shows a set of "stocks", after which the inn, and the road, are named . As you can see on the picture, the man is locked in the "stocks" as a form of punishment because he has committed a crime. The people in the stocks would have rotten vegetables thrown at them, or they were sometimes whipped.

23. Take great care crossing the road in front of "The Whipping Stocks" then follow the path (behind the hedge at this point) to the right along Stocks Lane. Pass Radbroke Hall (Barclays Bank) on the left, and, after the last of its driveways, (nearly ¼ mile) take the public footpath on the left, running along the edge of a field.

Escape Route: To return to the starting point continue along the lane for just over half a mile.

24. Avoid the two stiles off to the left, but at the second one, bear right across the field to the left of the hedge.

☺ The hedge contains mainly hawthorns. As you may guess, they have sharp thorns. In Autumn, they have bright red berries, called "haws". The berries attract many small birds which feed on them through the cold, winter months when there is little else to eat.

25. At the end of the field go through the gap in the hedge and keep straight ahead. The path soon becomes a farm trackway enclosed between hedges. Follow this as it bears around to the right, avoiding the stile to the left.

☺ This trackway is used by farmers. Perhaps you can see the marks of a tractor on the ground, or horses' hoofprints. The hedges are mainly hawthorns, but there are also nettles, ivy and tall, pink flowers called rosebay willow herb. The hedges provide shelter and homes for many wild animals like field mice and rabbits, and also small birds like sparrows and robins.

26. At the end of the track bear right along the lane. There is an open field on the right, and woodland on the left which is sometimes used as a caravan site. After the woods there are wide, open fields. Take the track to the left, the right leads only to a farmhouse.

☺ The crops change in the fields annually. Wheat, potatoes and sweet corn are often grown in Cheshire, and sometimes greens, such as cabbage or sprouts. The fields are often left as grass, to feed cows and sheep. If there is a crop in the field, can you tell what it is?

27. **The track crosses over a stream, and, soon after, bears right towards "Newhall Farm". Continue past the haybarn, then follow the drive round to the left.**

Q: The brick barn on your left is very old. When was it built?

A: 1711. The date can be seen over a door towards the back of the building. You can tell that many doors and windows in the barn have been bricked up as the bricks used are a slightly different colour.

28. **Continue along the drive and go through the five-barred gate straight ahead, crossing the field to a stile in the hedge. Alternatively, continue along the driveway and bear left at the end.**

Q: What is the date on the brick house opposite the stile?

A: 1937

29. **Head left along the lane, which will return you to the starting point at the crossroads.**

Over Peover checklist

☐ A HORSE

☐ A COW

☐ A HORSE CHESTNUT TREE

☐ A DUCK OR COOT

☐ A "SATELLITE DISH"

☐ A TRACTOR

☐ A GREENHOUSE

☐ A CHURCH TOWER

☐ A RABBIT

☐ A WHITE FARMHOUSE

☐ A WATER PUMP

☐ A GOLD CLOCK

Overton Hill

The first part of the walk offers views over the Mersey estuary, Frodsham, Ellesmere Port and towards Liverpool. It is certainly a very interesting sight, but may not be what you want to look at on a day out. It can be avoided by doing only the second part of the walk, through very attractive woodlands, along the early stages of the long distance footpath, the Sandstone Trail.

Starting point:	Beacon Hill car park (SJ519766). From Frodsham take the B5152 Delamere road. After $^3/4$ mile bear right along Manley road, signed "Mersey View 1 mile". After $1/2$ mile bear right along Simons Lane, signed for the golf course. There is a suitable lay-by on the right, but the main car park is further along, well-signed, also on the right.
By rail:	The nearest station is at Frodsham, a mile away. It is an uphill climb through houses.
Distance:	Entire route: 3 miles
Terrain:	Footpaths and short distances along quiet lanes. Some easy climbing over stepped sandstone, which can be avoided by using the second escape route. (Note: All escape routes use footpaths crossing the vast golf course. If you consider this unsafe, then stick to the entire route.)
Maps:	OS Landranger 117
Public Toilets:	None
Refreshments:	Nowhere in the vicinity
Pushchairs:	Not suitable at all

1.   **From main car park, bear left along the lane, downhill.**

Escape Route: To cut a large corner off the walk and avoid the industrial views, bear right from the car park, slightly uphill. After a short way take the footpath on the left, signed for "Alvanley". The path leads downhill, then across the golf course. Follow the occasional direction posts across the fairway, then between gorse bushes and down into the woods. Here bear left and go down the steps. Continue from direction 11.

2.   **After a short way look for the footpath on the left, signed "Bellemont & Frodsham". Follow the driveway, slightly uphill.**

Q: The gate next to the footpath has the name of a house on it. What is the name?

A: "Overton Cottage".

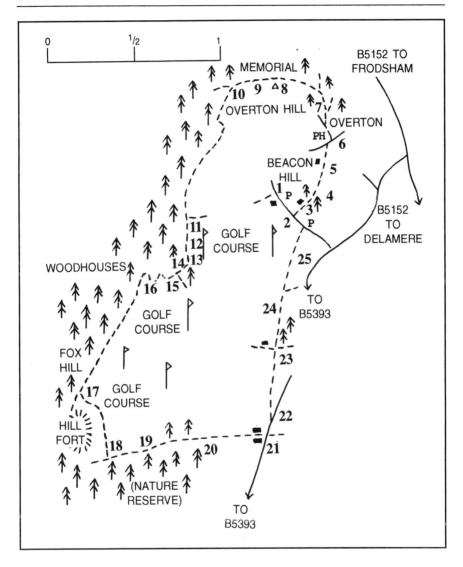

3. **When the drive bears left to the house, keep straight ahead along the grassy path.**

☺ Notice the old lamp post on the right. The path now passes between many thick bushes, most of which are prickly, including holly and hawthorn, and watch out for the nettles!

4. **Go through the five-barred gate. Cross the hotel driveway and continue straight ahead, with a wooden fence on the right. The path leads downhill, around the hotel gardens.**

☺ There are views, on the right, over the houses of Frodsham, and on the left are the grounds of a hotel, with many trees and rhododendron bushes.

5. **Follow the main path, which is fairly well-trodden. After the woods, pass in front of the bungalow and continue to the road. Bear right, downhill.**

Q: What is the name of the pub on the left?

A: "The Belle Monte".

("The Belle Monte" has a beer garden and family room)

6. **Bear left, passing the front of the pub. Look on the right, after the car park, for a narrow path leading downhill between bushes and trees. Follow this, bearing left almost immediately. Keep to the upper path at all times.**

☺ These are mixed woods with many oak trees and holly bushes. Ivy grows on some of the tree trunks, and over the ground in places. There are also blackberry bushes with their long, prickly stems; and bilberries, short bushes with light green leaves and black/purple berries in the autumn.

7. **Keep left along the upper path to the tall, stone monument. If you have missed the monument it should come into view, high up on the left. Take any of the small pathways which climb uphill towards it.**

☺ **(AT THE MONUMENT)** This monument is built of sandstone blocks, and is a memorial to the men from Frodsham (below) who died in the First and Second World Wars. From here there are views over the River Mersey as it makes its way towards the sea. If you look to the right you should be able to make out where the River Weaver joins the Mersey. You may be able to see the Manchester Ship Canal which runs below, between the Mersey and the motorway.

Close to the monument is a diagram showing all the things that can be seen and their distance from here. The cathedral in Liverpool, for example.

Q: Snowdon is the highest mountain in England and Wales. How far away is it from here?

A: 58½ miles.

Q: Chester is the capital city of Cheshire. How far away is it?

A: 9½ miles.

8. From the monument, continue along the cliff-top path, with the cliff on your right, passing in front of the hotel on your left. (Take care of the cliff edge.) Follow the path between the bushes and brambles. Keep to the upper path.

☺ After a short distance there should be many colourful trees below you, and there are now fields and marshes between the motorway and the river.

9. The path eventually drops slightly into the woods. Keep ahead on the upper path, with the fence on your left.

☺ The golf course, on your left, will remain in sight for some time and you will probably see people playing.

The trees here are mainly oaks, from which acorns come. Look for squirrels, who like to eat acorns and can often be seen running along the branches and tree trunks.

10. Cross the wooden "bridges" and continue ahead, keeping to the left. After some way the path drops through gorse bushes and trees to a stile on the left. Avoid this and follow the steps downhill and around to the left.

Escape Route: To return to the car park, bear left over the stile and follow the occasional posts across the golf course to an uphill path. This will bring you to a lane. Bear right, and the car park is just ahead on the left.

11. Always keep to the upper path. Go down a further set of steps called "Baker's Dozen".

Q: These steps are called "Baker's Dozen". How many are in a dozen? And how many steps are there?

A: A dozen is twelve, but in the "olden days" if you went into a baker's and asked for a dozen bread rolls, he would have given you twelve plus an extra one, making thirteen. (It probably wouldn't work today, but you could try it!)

12. Take care clambering down the sandstone outcrop, and continue down the further steps.

☺ This path is part of a long distance path called the "Sandstone Trail". On the left you should be able to see a "cliff" of sandstone rock, with trees growing on the top and hanging over. Can you see their roots clinging to the rock?

In the Autumn, when the leaves fall, they gather in piles on the ground. Hedgehogs like to curl up among the warm, dry leaves beneath hedges or bushes. If you have a bonfire, before lighting it, you should check that no hedgehogs have crawled underneath as many die this way. Hedgehogs are well known for their prickly backs. If they are frightened, they can roll into a ball and be safe from wild animals or dogs.
Have you noticed that in the Spring there are no leaves on the ground. What

happens to all the leaves that fall in the Autumn? They rot and break down, turning eventually into soil, which will feed other plants and trees. In nature, nothing is wasted.

13. **Continue down more steps. At the bottom the path bears to the right. Continue to the sign post.**

🙂 **(AT THE SIGNPOST)** The worn sandstone rock on the right is called "Jacob's Ladder" because it is like a stone staircase, and many people climb it. Can you see the foot-holes that have worn in the stone? Sandstone is very soft and wears away easily. This type of wearing away is called "erosion" and can be a problem, as numerous human feet can badly damage footpaths and work has to be done to repair them. This kind of repair work to the countryside is called "conservation" and people who do it, and care for the countryside, are called "conservationists".

14. **From the signpost, bear left, signed for Helsby. The path heads slightly uphill, with the rock-face visible on the left.**

🙂 If you look over to the left of the path you should be able to see a small cave high in the "cliff". Can you make out the foot-holes where people have climbed to it? Don't you try, it is very dangerous. You can see the sandy red colour of the sandstone, which, as its name suggests, is made up of thousands of grains of sand.

15. **Continue up the path, cobbled in places. Avoid the stile on the left and continue ahead to the rocky outcrop, signed for the Sandstone Trail. The path now ascends the outcrop by a series of worn "steps". It is not difficult, but take care of the drop on the right.**

Escape Route: To shorten the route, or to avoid the rocky climb, bear left over the stile and make your way through the bushes to a further stile. Keep straight ahead across the golf course. At first there is a hedge on the left. Continue to the sign post, then bear right. Keep straight ahead to a stile near the corner of the field. Follow the edge of the field towards the farm buildings. Continue straight through the farmyard, passing the farmhouse on the left (with a waterpump outside the door) and continue along the drive to the footpath on the left. Continue from direction 24.

16. **At the top of the rocky outcrop, continue along the main path. The golf course, on the left, should be kept in sight at all times. Many minor paths lead off into the trees.**

🙂 The trees here are still mainly oaks, but there are holly bushes, with dark green, prickly leaves. There is also bracken which is the tall, fern-like plant that turns dry and brown in the Winter.

On the golf course you should be able to see large holes filled with sand. These

Looking over the golf course towards Beacon Hill

are called "bunkers" and the golfers try to avoid them as it is difficult to hit a ball out of the sand. The coloured flags mark the holes that the golfers aim for.

17. **Bear left with the fence. The path leads slightly uphill through trees and undergrowth. Do not go onto the golf course. The fence continues fairly close on the left.**

😊 The golf course is now left behind for the time being, and you will see fields instead, probably with cows grazing.

The land rising on the right was once part of a hillfort, though nothing remains except these steep banks. These would have protected small wooden huts, which were homes, thousands of years ago.
There are still many oak trees in this part of the woods, but there are also birch trees. They have white trunks and diamond-shaped leaves. Look for toadstools. They can often be found growing under birches. If you see any, look, but do not touch, as many toadstools and mushrooms are poisonous.

18. **After some way the path rejoins the main Sandstone Trail. Bear left along this and keep the fence in sight on the left.**

😊 The trees are mostly birches now, and there is more of the fern-like bracken growing beneath them. Can you see a bird's nest in the branches of the trees?

In the Autumn or Winter, when the leaves have fallen, they are easy to spot. In the Spring, birds build new nests and then the female lays eggs. One bird, usually the mother, will sit on the eggs at all times to keep them warm. When the chicks hatch, the parent birds will bring them food until they are old enough to look after themselves.

Some birds, like the black and white magpie, eat other birds' eggs, and, occasionally, small chicks. Squirrels sometimes do the same. Magpies, once they find a mate, usually stay together for life. If you see a magpie, take a look around, there will probably be another nearby. Magpies have a habit of stealing bright, shiny objects, and taking them back to their nests.

19. **After a short way the Sandstone Trail path (marked by the footprint signs) bears off to the right, but keep straight ahead with the fence. Soon the fence will become lost, temporarily, in the trees and bracken. Continue straight ahead along the main path, leading slightly uphill, and rejoin the fence.**

☺ Amongst the birch trees there are a few rowan trees. These have orange-red berries in the Autumn and Winter. Can you spot any?

20. **Soon the path levels and crosses fields, with an occasional hedgerow on both sides. Go through the old five-barred gate and continue along the track between the houses.**

Q: On the right is a pair of semi-detached houses; that means they are joined together. How many chimneys are there on the roof?

A: Three.

21. **Bear left along the lane. There are well-trodden grass verges along both sides of the road.**

Q: On the left, almost hidden in the bushes, is the name of a house on a sign. What is the name of the house?

A: "Shepherd's Cottage".

22. **After a short way climb the stile on the left, signed for "Beacon Hill". Bear diagonally right, towards the transmitters on the hill.**

☺ On the left are the woods through which you have just walked. In the Autumn they are very colourful, and a popular place for walkers. There isn't far to go now.

23. **Climb the stile and cross the farm driveway to the path opposite.**

24. **Follow the footpath, avoiding the stile to the right.**

Q: Over the wire mesh fence on the right, there are often sheep grazing. A young sheep is called a lamb, but do you know what male and female sheep are called?

A: The female is called a "ewe" and the male is called a "ram".

☺ On the left there are views over the River Mersey, which is very wide here, on the last part of its journey to the sea. On the other side of the water is Liverpool. You should also be able to see the golf course again.

25. Pass the edge of the golf course and at the lane bear left, uphill, for the main car park.

Overton Hill checklist

☐ A COLOURED FLAG

☐ A SQUIRREL

☐ A PERSON WITH A RUCKSACK

☐ A BLACK AND WHITE COW

☐ A RABBIT HOLE

☐ AN ACORN

☐ A MUSHROOM OR TOADSTOOL

☐ A HORSE

☐ SOMEONE IN CHEQUERED TROUSERS PLAYING GOLF

☐ A TREE WITH RED BERRIES IN AUTUMN OR WHITE BLOSSOM IN SPRING

𝒫*eckforton*

This has to be one of the finest walks in Cheshire. A peaceful stroll through the gentle Peckforton hills, in the shadow of two of Cheshire's most impressive monuments: the castles of Beeston and Peckforton. Sit outside at "The Pheasant Inn", overlooking the Cheshire Plain; make your own candle (if you're under 14!) at the Cheshire Workshops; see the haunted bridge; the stone elephant and idyllic village scenes. A memorable and varied day out.

Starting point:	Sandstone Trail car park, near Beeston Castle (SJ540590). Head for Beeston Castle which is well-signed and visible for miles around. Bear west from the A49, passing through Beeston village. The car park is on the left immediately before the castle. (Beeston Castle car park further along is for visitors to the castle only.)
	To make the route shorter, there are a few parking spaces along Stone House Lane, (running between the villages of Peckforton and Beeston.) Park at your own discretion. Begin the walk by bearing left down Horsley Lane and join the route after direction 5.
Distance:	Entire route from Beeston – 5½ miles
Terrain:	Good paths and trackways, some gentle climbing through the Peckforton Hills.
Maps:	OS Landranger 117
Public Toilets:	No public toilets at all. Facilities at Beeston Castle, "Pheasant Inn", Cheshire Workshops for patrons only.
Refreshments:	Usually a mobile cafe and shop in Sandstone Trail car park; "Pheasant Inn", Higher Burwardsley; Cheshire Workshops, Higher Burwardsley, restaurant/tea-room.
Pushchairs:	From the second suggested starting point, the route is navigable for pushchairs. The return from Peckforton village is along a lane, but it does have wide grass verges for much of the way. The escape routes are not suitable for pushchairs.

1.   **From the Sandstone Trail car park near Beeston Castle, take the footpath alongside the gates of the car park, leading away from the lane, with the stone wall of Beeston Castle on your right.**

☺ On your right are the grounds of Beeston Castle which was built nearly 800 years ago by the Sixth Earl of Chester. Later there will be better views. **(SEE 'OTHER PLACES OF INTEREST' AT THE END OF THE WALK.)** There is supposed to be buried treasure hidden in the grounds, probably down the very deep well.

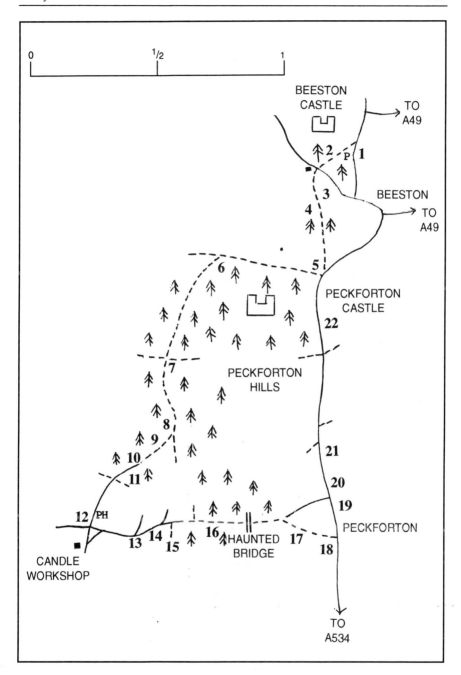

2. The path leads into an area of woodland, at which point it bears away from the wall and crosses the middle of the woods, leading downhill to Tattenhall Lane. Take great care crossing. (It is usually fairly quiet, but has a tight bend to the right.) Take the footpath to the left of "Tabernacle Cottage" opposite, signed for Grindley Brook.

Q: What kind of animal is on the weather vane on the roof of the cottage?

A: A dog.

3. Follow the wide, sandy pathway towards the trees. This is part of the Sandstone Trail and is well-trodden.

☺ Ahead, rising out of the trees, is Peckforton Castle **(OPEN TO THE PUBLIC: SEE 'OTHER PLACES OF INTEREST' AT END OF WALK FOR DETAILS OF OPENING ETC.)** It is much more recent than Beeston Castle, having been built 150 years ago as a "stately home". It was made to look much older and situated so that it could be seen for miles, and would give views over the owner's surrounding fields. Recently it has been used as the setting for films and television programmes, including "Robin Hood", "Doctor Who", "Sherlock Holmes" and "The Chronicles of Narnia".

Peckforton Castle

4. **At the end of the field enter the fringe of woodland, descending the steps and crossing the small stream. Continue straight ahead and follow the path along the edge of the field, with the hedge on your right.**

☺ Close to the stream there are tall, waterside plants, like nettles, dock and thistles, and flowers which attract butterflies in the summer months.

(FROM HIGHER UP THE FIELD) If you turn around you have a good view of Beeston Castle on its rocky hilltop. In 1642, during the Civil War, when the government opposed King Charles I, it was the scene of much fighting and the damage can still be seen. It is one of Cheshire's most visited historical monuments.

5. **Bear right along the tarmac driveway.**

Q: The first building you pass is "Moat House Barn". It is on the right with two round windows looking over this driveway. What animal is on the weather vane on the building behind the house?

A: A cockerel.

6. **Bear left along the wide trackway, through trees, leading slightly uphill onto the Peckforton estate.**

☺ These woods are part of the grounds of Peckforton Castle. There is a Fire Warning on the left because,in very hot weather, when there are dry leaves and twigs on the ground, fires can easily be started. There are many different types of trees here, including oak, holly and sweet chestnut. Sweet chestnut trees have long leaves with jagged edges, and are related to the Horse Chestnut.

Q: Do you know what the fruit of the Horse Chestnut tree is called?

A: A conker.

If you walk quietly you may see squirrels on the ground, looking for food, or in the branches of overhanging trees. Unless you are very quiet, they will probably see you first.
At some places along the path there are rabbit holes in the sandy banks. Wild rabbits are shy creatures, and will dart for cover as you approach.
Look on the ground for fircones and see if you can tell which trees they have fallen from. In some places along the path you will be able to see between the trees, **(ON THE RIGHT)** across the flat Cheshire Plain, towards the hills of Wales.

7. **At the crossroads of footpaths continue ahead, signed for Bulkeley Hill.**

Escape Route: Bear left, signed for "Peckforton Lodge". Follow the footpath over the hill and join the driveway leading down to the lodge. Go through the archway and bear left along the lane, then continue with direction 22 and onwards.

☺ Soon you will pass a conifer plantation on the right. Can you tell the difference between these trees and most of the other trees in the woods around you? The conifers have dark needles instead of leaves, and tall, straight trunks or boughs. They grow more quickly than most British trees. They are grown for their wood, to make furniture or paper, and for Christmas trees. Fir, pine and larch are all conifers.

8. At the next junction keep straight ahead, signed for Burwardsley, down a sandy trackway.

*Escape Route:*Take the steps uphill to the left, signed for Bulkeley Hill. At the next junction, climb the stile, signed for Hill Lane & Peckforton village, and continue through the trees. At the trackway bear left and follow direction 16 and onwards.

9. Follow the path as it leads downhill through overhanging trees and go through the gate at the end of the drive.

Q: What is the name of the first farm on the right?

A: "Spring House Farm".

10. Continue along the lane.

Q: What is the word for a number of burrows where several rabbits live?

A: A warren.

☺ On the hill, on the right, there are many rabbit holes in the soft, sandy soil, and gorse bushes which have long prickles and yellow flowers. Hares are related to rabbits, but much larger. They live in the middle of thick bushes, like gorse.

Q: On the left is a cottage of brick and sandstone, painted white. It is named after a flower. What is it called?

A: "Lilac Cottage".

11. Keep to the lane, avoiding footpaths on both sides, arriving at "The Pheasant Inn" on the left.

(There are tables outside, fine views for miles, a fountain and, of special interest to children, a playground and a telescope looking out over the Cheshire Plain. The inn is very popular with walkers doing the Sandstone Trail.)

Q: What is pictured on the inn sign?

A: A pheasant, which is a type of bird.

☺ "The Pheasant Inn" is very old, and has been a pub for at least 350 years, although its name has changed. Can you tell where the original building has been extended?

Q: You may notice models of an insect on the walls. Which insect?

A: Butterflies. Some of them are almost hidden in the ivy.

For the candle workshops bear left from "The Pheasant Inn" and continue straight across at the crossroads. The workshops are on the right. They are open daily from 10 to 5. Admission is free and food and toilets are available. There are demonstrations of candle-making, glassblowing etc. Children over 5 can make their own candles. Afterwards return to the crossroads by "The Pheasant Inn" to continue.

12. **From the inn, bear left onto the lane, and left at the crossroads, passing the 'phone box. Turn left again, signed as a dead end. The lane winds slightly uphill between high hedges and overhanging trees. At the fork bear right, still uphill.**

Q: What is the name of the farm on the left?

A: "Rockhouse Farm". It is built mainly of sandstone. Shortly you will be able to see the rock as the lane cuts into it. It is usually sandy red, like the farm-house, but here it is covered with moss and lichen.

13. **Keep straight ahead, passing a whitewashed cottage on the right, bearing a plaque saying "Elephant Track". Continue along the trackway, signed for Bulkeley Hill.**

☺ This is not called the Elephant Track because elephants walk along here, but because there were once cottages at the other end of the track and outside one was a life-size stone elephant.

14. **Keep ahead. The road degenerates into a stony trackway, signed for Peck-forton & Stonehouse Lane. The path is level and passes between ferns and hedges, before woods begin on either side.**

☺ You may pass a field with horses along the trackway and there may be Highland Cattle grazing. They have long horns and woolly coats. They originally came from Scotland, which explains their name.

15. **Avoid the footpath to the left, and continue ahead.**

☺ You should pass another plantation of conifers. Can you recognise them?

Look for pheasants, like the bird on the inn sign, and rabbits.

16. **The path soon begins to descend. Go under the sandstone bridge and continue ahead.**

☺ **(AT THE BRIDGE)** This is called the Haunted Bridge and was once part of the main driveway of Peckforton Castle, which is now hidden in the trees. Horses and carriages would drive along here from the gatehouse to the castle. It is supposedly haunted by a servant woman from the castle.

(A morbid note for adults: she is supposed to carry a severed head beneath her arm.)

(Pushchairs continue down the trackway and bear left at the bottom. Continue from direction 20.)

17. **Take the stile to the right, immediately after the haunted bridge, heading straight across the field towards a fringe of trees, with cottages and farmhouses visible beyond. There are several stiles close together. Follow the path which leads, at last, through an area of young conifers. Bear left along the stony driveway to the lane.**

☺ This is the village of Peckforton. Most of the houses are very old. On the left is a thatched cottage with black and white walls. Notice how most of the other cottages are very similar, with the same square chimneys, windows, and colours. Lord Tollemache, who lived in the castle, owned all these houses and improved them for the villagers. This is when the diamond shaped windows were put in.

18. **Bear left along the pavement.**

☺ Look for the elephant. **(CLEARLY VISIBLE FROM THE PAVEMENT, IN A GARDEN ON THE LEFT.)** It is carved from stone and is carrying a castle on its back. It was made by a stonemason who was working on Peckforton Castle, when it was being built. It stood outside his cottage near the Haunted Bridge, and when the cottage was pulled down, it was moved here. It is thought the castle was intended as a beehive, though it was probably never used as such. A possible explanation for this figure is that the family who owned the surrounding area several hundred years ago had an elephant and a castle on their "coat of arms" or Family Emblem.

19. **Continue along the lane.**

☺ After the stone elephant there is a small orchard **(ALSO ON THE LEFT)** with apple and pear trees.

20. **The pavement ends at the next cottage, but for most of the way there are grass verges on one side or the other.**

☺ On the right there are several more apple trees, and in the hedgerows other fruits are growing, such as blackberries and elderberries.

Q: Look for the tall, brick chimneys of the next cottage. How many does it have?

A: Four, all in a row in the middle of the roof.

Soon Beeston Castle comes into view, on its rocky hilltop. It looks a very **(VERY)** long way away, but it isn't as far as it seems.
Look for "Castle Cottage" on the right, with a water pump in its garden which once was used to pump water out of the ground when there were no taps or running hot water! A tin bath in front of the fire was the best that was available.

21. Continue along the lane to the gatehouse of Peckforton Castle.

☺ This is the entrance to the grounds of Peckforton Castle. A gatekeeper would have lived in the house to the right of the archway, to open the gates and admit visitors. **(See 'Other Places of Interest' .)**

22. Continue along the lane after Peckforton Lodge for just under half a mile. Bear left along a driveway to the left. (This is signed as a private road, but it applies only to vehicles. It is a public footpath.) After a short way, take the footpath off to the right, heading back towards Beeston Castle. Return across the road and through the woods, bearing right at the stone wall, back to the car park.

The stone elephant, Peckforton village

Other Places of Interest

Beeston Castle

Open daily from April to October, 10am to 6pm. A short climb through the pleasant woodlands of Beeston Crag to the castle, from which there are unspoiled panoramic views in all directions. There is also a museum depicting the history of the castle and its role in the civil war.

Peckforton Castle

Building began in 1844, to a design of a 12th century castle. It is open daily from Easter to September, 10am to 6pm. The main entrance is through the archway at Peckforton Lodge, near to the village of Peckforton. The castle is partially moated and in the central courtyard cats and hens live happily together. A history of the castle is given by animated figures, such as the gossiping verger in the chapel. The castle has provided the setting for many films and TV programmes. At weekends there are usually activities for children. Phone for details: 01829 260930. Cafe and refreshments available. Toilets & disabled facilities.

Stop Press! The castle has recently gone on the market so its future is uncertain.

Peckforton checklist

- [ ] A CASTLE
- [ ] A RED CAR
- [ ] A STREAM
- [ ] A TRACTOR
- [ ] A RABBIT'S BURROW
- [ ] A SQUIRREL
- [ ] A TELESCOPE
- [ ] A STONE BRIDGE
- [ ] A COW
- [ ] A THATCHED COTTAGE
- [ ] AN ELEPHANT
- [ ] A STONE ARCHWAY

Redesmere and Capesthorne

This walk is entirely flat and includes some of the Cheshire Plain's most popular attractions. Redesmere has a wide variety of birdlife, so don't forget to bring some brown bread. Capesthorne Hall is one of the county's most impressive stately homes and is open to the public at weekends in Summer, and occasional days throughout the week.

Starting point:	Car park at Redesmere Lake, Siddington (SJ848713) off the A34 between Congleton and Alderley Edge.
Buses:	From Macclesfield, Manchester, Northwich and Knutsford to Monk's Heath. From here it is a half mile walk along the roadside footpath.
Distance:	3 miles
Terrain:	Flat all the way, over fields and along lanes. Possibly some mud in wet weather.
Maps:	OS Landranger 118
Public Toilets:	None. (The public toilets near Redesmere, marked on some OS maps, have now been demolished.)
Refreshments:	Tea-room at Capesthorne Hall, for visitors only. Nearby – Matthews Garden Centre, Monks Heath – cafe and children's play area.

1. **From the car park, turn right along the lane with the lake on your left.**

Redesmere is a well-known local beauty spot with ample parking along its southern shore. There are good views across the lake.

☺ Redesmere means "reedy lake". There are many birds including swans, mallards, coots, herons and Canada geese. Can you recognise any of them?

2. **Pass an area of woodland on the left, after the lake, then take the signed footpath on the left across open fields.**

☺ There may be horses or donkeys grazing in this field. Donkeys do not like to be alone, so they are often kept in pairs, or with a horse companion.

3. **Climb the stile and bear left through the woods, crossing a wooden bridge over a stream. The short stretch ahead can be muddy in bad weather, though work has been done to improve this. Go through the gate and pass the yacht club on the left, then veer right onto the stony trackway. Follow it along the length of the lake.**

Q: What shape is the flag on the sign at the gate of the Yacht Club?

A: Triangular. **(THE SIGN IS IN THE HEDGE TO THE RIGHT OF THE GATE.)**

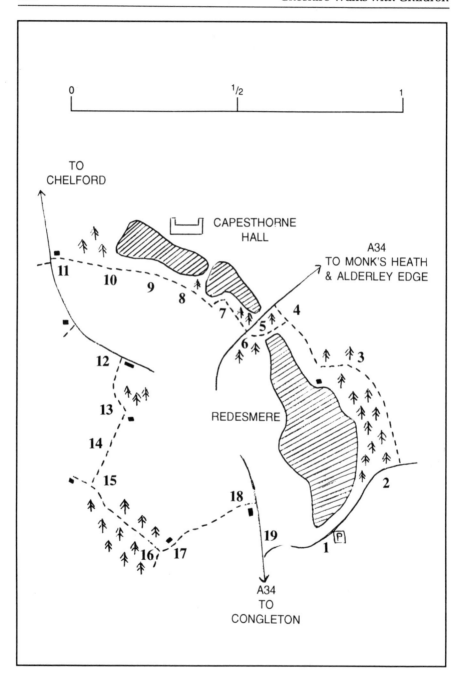

4. At the end of the lake bear left over the grass and cross a small footbridge. Continue along the path which runs along the foot of the lake.

☺ There are good views from here along the lake towards the yacht club. Perhaps there are boats or windsurfers on the water. Reeds and bulrushes grow in the shallow water around the edge of the lake. The long brown part of the bulrush contains hundreds of tiny seeds which are blown away by the wind.

5. Continue over another footbridge and follow the path to the main road.

☺ The stream is the overflow from Redesmere. After heavy rain the lake will overflow into this stream. The water goes from here into a series of further lakes which you will soon see.

6. Cross the road carefully as there are bends in both directions. Follow the path, signed for Mill Lane, across the opposite field, running along the edge of a farmed field.

☺ The path runs around the edge of a farmed field which may be left to grass or be growing a crop, such as wheat, for which Cheshire is famous. In the woods (ON THE RIGHT) there are rabbits, hares and possibly foxes and badgers. Be alert and you may see one, although they are timid. The trees nearest the fence are younger and smaller than those behind.

7. Approach the first pond with the boathouse on the opposite bank, and bear left to the stile. After the stile keep right, passing the pond and coming to a further lake, over which is Capesthorne Hall.

☺ These lakes are not natural, but were made by damming the stream that runs out of Redesmere, so that the water flooded the lowest parts of the fields. This was done by the people who lived at Capesthorne Hall. You may be able to see (ON THE OPPOSITE SIDE OF THE WATER, TOWARDS THE BEGINNING OF THE LAKE) a brick and stone column, like a tall gatepost, standing in the middle of the field. This is to mark the spot where the old hall used to stand before it was demolished and the present house built.

Capesthorne Hall is the home of the Bromley-Davenport family, who were wealthy landowners. The hall is built of brick with various turrets and towers. The front is longer than Buckingham Palace. All but the rear of the building, which is 280 years old, was destroyed by fire and has been rebuilt. It looks very grand in daylight, but at night, beware, for the hall is said to be haunted! A mysterious Lady in Grey roams through the rooms and along the dark corridors of the old building . . .

Forty years ago, William Bromley-Davenport was awoken by a sound; a scratching at his window. He opened the curtains and saw a hand hanging in mid-air, with the fingers scraping at the glass. Very bravely, he opened the window but the hand disappeared. It has never reappeared , but the tale survives.

8.   Continue along the lake towards the ornamental bridge.

Q: How many arches are there on the bridge?

A: Five.

The ornamental bridge

9.   Go through the kissing gate and continue along the lakeside.

☺ Over the water you can see the side of the hall and the gardens. The pathway between the lawns leads to the hall's private chapel where the Bromley-Davenport family have been buried in the crypt. A procession of ghostly figures is said to haunt the crypt.

10. Continue past the lake and follow the gravel trackway towards the gate.

☺ In the trees **(ON THE RIGHT)** is the old saw mill **(NOW USED BY "DINGHYCRAFT")**. It was worked until 1936, using waterpower to turn the circular cutting saw. It provided all the wood for the estate, for fences and buildings.

11. **Bear left along Mill Lane. (Wide grass verges on both sides.)**

☺ **(AT PARK FARM, ON THE BEND OF THE LANE.)** This is Park Farm, and was once part of the Capesthorne Estate, growing crops for the family at the hall. Above the door is the family coat of arms, or emblem.

12. **Follow the lane. Take the stile on the right, just before the brick cottages. Cross the field towards the woods and continue with the woods on your left.**

☺ These are mixed woods, and have many different types of trees. Some of the trees have berries in the Autumn. Elderberries have purple/black clusters of small berries, rowans have bright orange berries that turn red and hawthorns also have red berries. They provide food for the birds when it is scarce.

13. **Climb the stile in the hedge and bear left across the field. As you round the edge of the woods, a farmhouse should come into view. The next stile is to the right of the house.**

☺ **(AT THE STILE)** To the right is a small pond, surrounded by rushes and reeds, with many overhanging trees. There may be ducks here. Ducks have flat "webbed" feet which act like flippers and help them to swim. The female ducks are usually brown, while the males have green and blue patterns on their feathers.

14. **Climb the stile and continue straight ahead along the edge of the field, with the hedge on your right.**

☺ **(A SHORT WAY ACROSS THE FIELD INDICATE TO THE RIGHT)** Over the flat fields you should be able to see a huge satellite dish. This is the Jodrell Bank Radio Telescope, but you cannot look through it. The dish points to the sky and can track objects moving in space.

15. **Climb the next stile and bear left along a grassy trackway. In a short way the track is barred by a five-bar gate, but the footpath continues to the right of the gate. Go through the undergrowth into the woods.**

☺ This path is also used by horse riders. See if you can see any hoofprints on the ground.

A stream runs through the woods, down in the trees to the right. You may be able to hear the rushing of its water.

16. **Where the path divides, bear left and keep to the main trackway.**

☺ There is a house on the left, through the trees, with a thatched roof. Thatched roofs sometimes have to be replaced and the person who does this is called a "thatcher". It is now a name, like Baker and Woodman. Have you heard the name Thatcher before?

17. **Pass the buildings on the left and follow the drive round to the right.**

☺ Some of the fields will be grass, but others may have wheat or corn in them.

Q: Which daily foods are made from wheat?
A: Bread, breakfast cereals, biscuits, among others.

18. **At the head of the drive pass farm buildings and bear right along the footpath of the main road.**

☺ **(ON THE LEFT AT THE TOP OF THE LANE)** This is the remains of an orchard. Among the fruit trees are damsons, a type of purple plum, used for making jam and wine; also elderberry trees and blackberry bushes.

(ON THE ROAD) Here there are more thatched cottages with white-painted brick walls.

Q: How many chimneys can you count on the cottages?
A: Four.

19. **Take the first left turning, taking care while crossing the main road. In a short distance the lane leads back to the car park at Redesmere.**

There are picnic tables on the left before the lake, in an enclosed area that once contained the public toilets. At the start of the lake there is a notice board with illustrations of all the birds that visit Redesmere.

Other places of Interest in the Area

Jodrell Bank Radio Telescope and Science Centre
Well-signed from the A535 between Chelford and Holmes Chapel. Working models of the radio telescope, planetarium, displays and exhibitions, attractive arboretum in the grounds, child-friendly science "games", cafe and toilets. Open daily from Easter to October. Weekends only through the winter.

Alderley Edge
See Alderley Edge route.

Redesmere & Capesthorne checklist

- [ ] A SILVER CAR
- [ ] A BOAT OR WINDSURFER
- [ ] A SWAN
- [ ] A DUCK
- [ ] A HORSE
- [ ] A COW
- [ ] BULRUSHES
- [ ] A WOODEN FOOTBRIDGE
- [ ] A STONE BRIDGE
- [ ] A TREE WITH BERRIES
- [ ] A BLACKBERRY BUSH
- [ ] A THATCHED ROOF

Risley Moss

Risley Moss, once the site of a munitions factory, is a nature reserve on the outskirts of Warrington. Peat was later cut from the area, but The Moss has since been purposely waterlogged to encourage moss growth and a wetland habitat. It is a haven for wildlife and an essential port of call for any amateur or junior naturalists. There is a visitor centre packed with information, helpful wardens on hand and various woodland hides, and it's all free! An excellent place to have a picnic, with picnic tables at various locations. Please note, however, that the Moss is closed on Fridays.

Starting point:	Risley Moss local nature reserve (SJ665920) which can be found a mile from junction 11 of the M62, just north-east of Warrington.
By rail:	Nearest station: Birchwood, on the Manchester to Liverpool line. It is then a walk of just over a mile.
Distance:	Entire route: a mere mile!
Terrain:	Flat gravel paths through woodland. Suitable for any weather.
Maps:	OS Landranger 109
	Map of reserve available from Visitor Centre.
Public Toilets:	At the Visitor Centre
Refreshments:	None in the immediate area.
Pushchairs:	An ideal circular route along well-maintained paths.

1. **Once through the main gates of the reserve, (the car park is well-signed) follow the paths to the Visitor Centre, visible through the trees.**

☺ Inside the Visitor Centre is information about the wildlife that you might see on your walk. There are large models of a dragonfly, frog, kingfisher and several other animals. How many can you recognise?

2. **Facing the Visitor Centre, bear left and then right, around the side of the centre.**

(Here you will find the first picnic site.)

3. **Take the first left turning.**

☺ This is a mixed wood, with different types of trees growing. Here they are mainly oak and ash trees, but there are also beech and prickly hawthorns.

☺ On the left is a viewing point over a small pond with duckweed floating on its

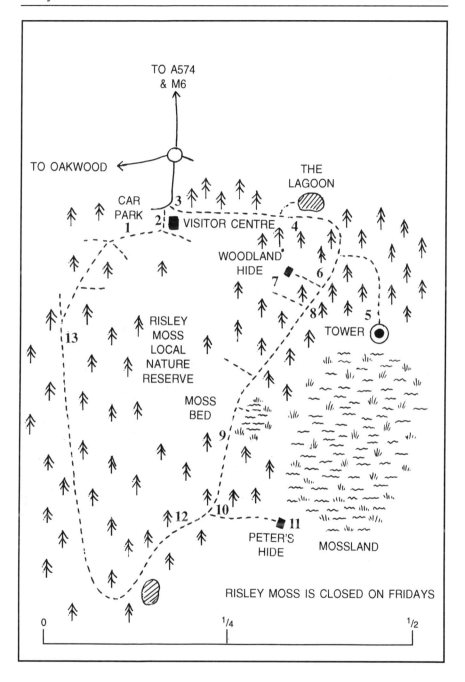

TO A574
& M6

TO OAKWOOD

THE
LAGOON

CAR
PARK
1

3

2 VISITOR CENTRE 4

WOODLAND
HIDE

7 6

8 5

TOWER

RISLEY
MOSS
LOCAL
NATURE
RESERVE

13

MOSS
BED

9

10

12

11

PETER'S
HIDE

MOSSLAND

RISLEY MOSS IS CLOSED ON FRIDAYS

0   1/4   1/2

surface, and rushes, brambles and reeds around its banks. These attract many insects like dragonflies and butterflies.

Further along the path there are many logs left to "decay". Rotten tree trunks provide homes for insects which can burrow into the soft, dead wood. Can you see fungus on some of the tree trunks?

4.   After the pond keep left, then bear right, signed for the Tower.

The Observation Tower

Ahead, you should see an observation tower. If you climb the steps into the tower there are views across an area of pools, swamps and undergrowthwhich is called "mossland". This is land that has been waterlogged by building ditches, and stopping rainwater draining away, so the soil is always wet. This makes the ground ideal for mosses and other plants that like moisture. The trees have been removed as they would "drink" too much water. Trees drink through their roots, which can spread under the ground for a very long way. A birch tree can absorb 30 gallons of water a day. That's 240 pints, which is about the same as two baths full almost to the top. The mossland attracts birds, butterflies and many other insects.

5.   Return the same way to the main path and bear left.

Can you see any trees which have berries in the late Summer and Autumn? Elderberry trees have clusters of small blackish-purple berries, rowans have bright red berries. The berries contain seeds which are carried away by birds and from which a new tree could grow.

6. **Take the next right turning, signed for the Woodland Hide.**

☺ This path leads to a "hide". This is a special building where you can sit and look out at wild animals and birds, without them seeing you. It is quite dark inside the hide. If you go in, keep quiet, so you do not disturb other people who may be trying to watch the animals. See if you can see any animals. Food is put out to attract birds to this area.

7. **Return the same way and bear right along the main path. Keep straight ahead and avoid all turnings.**

Escape Route: Take the next right turning, signed for the car park.

8. **Continue ahead, signed for Peter's Hide.**

The path passes through a grassy area where there are picnic tables.

☺ Look out for a wooden walkway to the left, where you can look over an area of moss, called sphagnum moss. It grows well in wet conditions. The mossland you could see from the tower is mainly of this type.

9. **Continue along the main path.**

☺ Many of the trees along the path here are very thin, because they are growing close together. There are many plants in the woods which could harm you. Never touch or eat wild berries or mushrooms, as they may be very poisonous. Animals may eat them, but that doesn't mean they are safe for people.

10. **Bear left, signed for Peter's Hide.**

☺ This hide looks over the mossland, over ferns and water. Many different types of birds can be observed, including magpies, ducks and gulls. Look for herons, which have long legs and can wade through water. Sit quietly for a few minutes and count how many birds you can see.

11. **Return to the main path and bear left.**

☺ You will soon pass another small pond on the left. Again this has green weeds on the surface, and reeds around its edges. Can you see birds or insects near the water?

12. **Follow the path as it bears around to the right.**

☺ You should see silver birch trees here. They have slim, silvery white trunks and diamond shaped leaves. There are often red-capped toadstools growing beneath.

(Ahead is another picnic site)

13. Keep to the main path which is signed for the car park. The Visitor Centre will soon come into view ahead. Bear left for the car park.

Risley Moss checklist

☐ A GIANT FROG

☐ A SQUIRREL

☐ A POND

☐ A BIRD'S FEATHER

☐ A BLACKBERRY BUSH

☐ A WOODEN BENCH

☐ A PERSON WALKING A DOG

☐ A PICNIC TABLE

☐ A DUCK

☐ A FALLEN TREE OR LOG

𝕾𝓽𝔂𝓪𝓵 𝓦𝓸𝓸𝓭𝓼

An excellent day out for children, especially if a visit to the mill is included. Along the River Bollin there are easy walks through attractive mixed woodland, carefully maintained by the National Trust. Ideal for any season.

Starting points:	**Routes A & B:** National Trust car park near Norcliffe Chapel, (SJ835835) off Altrincham Road, Styal (free). **Route C:** main car park, Quarry Bank Mill, Styal (free to NT members).
By rail:	Styal station. Bear right for Styal village.
Distances:	**Route A** – 3 miles. Entire route. **Route B** – 1.5 miles. Styal village and Western Woods. **Route C** – 1.5 miles. Southern Woods and Quarry Bank Mill.
Terrain:	Well-maintained pathways through the woods. Some uphill stretches.
Maps:	OS Landranger 109
Public Toilets:	Quarry Bank Mill
Refreshments:	Quarry Bank Mill
Pushchairs:	The *whole* route is difficult if not impossible for pushchairs, but there is good accessibility around the village and the mill area. The Western Woods are passable with some effort. A short and pleasant circuit of the Southern Woods can be made from the car park at Twinnies Bridge, off Styal Road (SJ839822)

ROUTES A & B: from Altrincham Rd car park, continue from (1) below. ROUTE C: from the main car park (Quarry Bank Mill), bear to the left (away from the entrance) and continue from Direction 5, (p 141).

1. From the National Trust car park on Altrincham Road, turn right along the road, passing allotments on the right, then bear right along the cobbled driveway that leads to Norcliffe Chapel.

☺ Over 200 years ago, an Irishman, Samuel Greg, built a cotton mill nearby, on the banks of the River Bollin. He later built homes for his workers. (**INDICATE FARM FOLD COTTAGES ON THE LEFT**). The cottages are simple, but well-kept.

(**A SHORT WAY AHEAD, IN AN ENCLOSURE ON THE LEFT, IS A HEADLESS CROSS.**) This is Styal Cross, believed to be at least 500 years old. It used to stand near the main road, but was damaged in a road accident and its remains were moved here to prevent further damage.

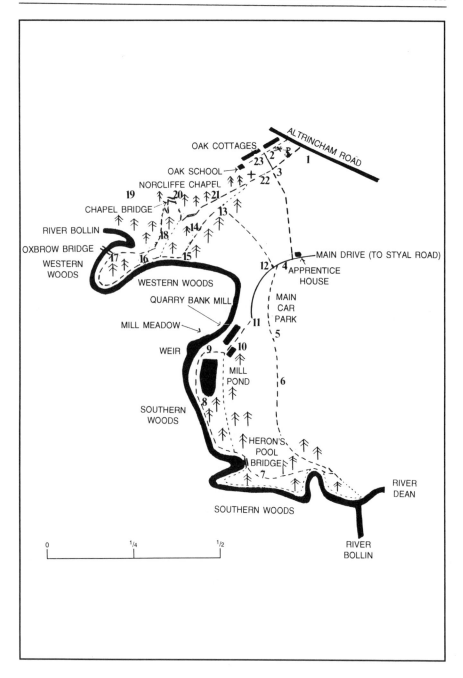

2. **Bear left after the cross, along a footpath and past a small pond.**

☺ Over on the left are more cottages which were made from a large barn to house the increasing number of mill workers. The building with a lantern over the door is Styal Chapel and was at one time a farm building where grain was stored. It was made into a church over 150 years ago.

3. **Continue straight across at the "crossroads" and follow the footpath.**

(The fields on either side of the path are leased to farmers by the National Trust and cows can often be seen here.)

Q: What are black and white cows called?

A: Friesians.

☺ **(INDICATE THE WHITE BUILDING VISIBLE AHEAD AND TO THE LEFT.)** This is the Apprentice House. Orphans were brought to work in the mill, and lived here. They ranged from nine to eighteen years old, and, in return for their work, were fed, clothed and given a basic education. Their lives, though much better than in the workhouses, were hard. They worked long hours, from six o'clock in the morning until seven o'clock at night. The Apprentice House was home to about 85 children at any one time, and they slept in large rooms with the girls on one side and the boys on the other.

(FOR ROUTE B: bear right along the drive and take the second footpath on the right, signed "to the woods" then follow directions 13 and onwards)

4. **Bear right along the driveway for a short way, and look for a gap in the wall on the left which leads to the main car park. Follow the path, with the cars on your left.**

☺ **(ON THE GRASS ON THE RIGHT, INDICATE THE LARGE IRON AXLE.)** This was part of the giant waterwheel from the mill which used the power of water to turn the mill machinery. It has now been replaced by a new wheel.

Route C starts here (see also page 139)

5. **Continue along the path to the far side of the car park, passing a small pond on the right. Take the stile to the left, crossing a rutted trackway, then a further stile leading onto farmed land. Continue ahead.**

☺ This path is known as the Apprentices' Path, because the children would walk along here every Sunday morning, to the church in Wilmslow.
Notice how the hedge **(ON THE RIGHT)** is made up of many different plants. It is mainly hawthorn, (which has sharp thorns), but there are also brambles (with prickly stems) and holly, (which has prickly leaves). Hedges like these make ideal places for wild animals to shelter and build nests.
Manchester Airport is close by and you may see and hear many planes taking off and landing.

6.   Go through the iron kissing gate and continue. The path is soon enclosed, with hawthorn hedges on either side, and, in a short way, becomes cobbled and leads downhill. Cross the stile and bear right, going through a metal gate into Styal Woods. Keep right, along Bluebell Bank.

☺ **(A SHORT WAY INTO THE WOODS)** Can you spot any willow trees in this part of the woods? They have long, thin leaves, and were grown here for their long, stem-like branches.

Q: Can you guess what for?

A: They were made into baskets.

7.   After a quarter of a mile, take the path uphill and cross Heron's Pool Bridge and continue left along the riverside path.

☺ The river here is wide and slow, and often brown, from the sandy mud it carries. In many places the bank has been supported, to prevent it collapsing, as the water steadily wears it away.

8.   Continue to the mill pond on the right.

☺ The large building ahead is Quarry Bank Mill, a cotton mill. Cotton comes from a plant, and is harvested as fluffy white balls, like cotton wool. These balls can be spun to make yarn (thick threads) which can then be made into clothes. The mill was built 200 years ago. Underneath it is a large waterwheel which is turned by the water from the River Bollin. The wheel was able to power the mill machines before electricity was invented.
This pond was once used to store water which was used to turn the waterwheel inside the mill. It is now a haven for wildlife, with bulrushes growing along its banks. How many birds or ducks can you see?
You can probably hear the great rushing of water ahead. **(ON THE BEND OF THE PATH, ON THE LEFT).** This is the weir which is used to control the level of water, so that there is always enough to power the waterwheel.

9.   Continue along the path, cross the bridge and bear left onto the main path towards the mill.

☺ **(INDICATE THE STREAM RUNNING ON THE LEFT OF THE MAIN PATH).** This stream is called the "head race". It is a channel of water, taken from the main river, which runs into the mill to the waterwheel.

(FROM THE MAIN PATH, SHORTLY BEFORE THE STEPS THAT LEAD DOWN TO THE MILL) Here you can see a "lock-gate" which can be raised or lowered to adjust the flow of water to the mill. To stop the waterwheel from turning, the lock gate is lowered and the water stops. The opposite gate is opened and the water flows back to the river.

10. Go down the steep steps into the cobbled courtyard by the mill buildings.

Here you will find the entrance to Quarry Bank Mill, a working museum which attracts visitors from all over the country. It has displays relating to cotton production and the chance to see the mill in action, with constantly clacking looms and spinning machines. It may not be suitable for very young children, but most youngsters find it quite interesting. Many local schools do projects about the mill so any information gleaned now may come in useful in the future. Tickets are available from the reception on the right, near the National Trust shop. To the left is the Mill Kitchen Cafe and Restaurant, and the public toilets.

For a better view of the weir, or to picnic, follow the path directly in front of the mill and bear left along a cobbled track to the mill meadow.

11. From the mill continue along the main driveway, leading uphill.

☺ As the business succeeded, the mill was extended several times. On the roof there is a small bell-tower which was used to call the villagers to work in the morning. In many mill villages someone went around, knocking on all the doors to wake everyone for work, because no-one had an alarm clock.

End of Route C: bear right up the slope or steps to the main car park.

☺ **(ON THE LEFT SHORTLY AFTER THE MILL IS THE GATEWAY TO A WHITE GEORGIAN HOUSE.)** This is Quarry Bank House, where Samuel Greg, the owner of the Mill lived with his family. While he was alive the mill was very profitable and he was able to open mills elsewhere. When he died his sons took over his business, but it was less successful.

12. Take the footpath on the left, signed "to the woods". Follow the path between hawthorn hedges, crossing a driveway at the middle point, and continue ahead into the woods.

Escape Route: To return to the Altrincham Road car park, turn right here and keep straight ahead

13. To continue with the route, bear left through the woods.

Q: How many of the different trees and bushes in the woods can you recognise?

A: Some of the more common varieties are:
Rhododendron bushes; Holly; Beech; Hawthorn; Oak; Sycamore

14. Follow the path and steps down to the river.

☺ Quarry Bank Mill is further along the river, and the water was used to turn a huge waterwheel which powered the mill machinery which wove thread into cotton cloth. Are you wearing something made from cotton?

Q: Does cotton come from an animal or a plant?

A: Cotton comes from a plant and is in fluffy balls, like cotton wool, when it is harvested. It is then spun into threads and made into cloth.

15. **At the river, bear right, crossing Kingfisher Bridge and continuing along the riverside path. When the path splits, keep left, close to the river. The path passes through an area of conifers.**

☺   These tall trees are called conifers or evergreens.

Q: What is an evergreen tree?
A: A tree which does not lose its leaves in Winter, unlike most British trees. They are often grown for their wood, to make furniture and paper.

16. **Follow the path around the bend of the river.**

☺   There are many birds and wild animals in the woods. If you keep very quiet and still for a few minutes you may see a squirrel running along the branches or on the ground, looking for food. They build homes out of leaves and twigs. These are called dreys and look like large birds' nests. If you look high up in the trees, you may see a drey.

Q: What do you think squirrels eat?
A: They eat nuts and seeds from the trees, like acorns and fircones, young green shoots and sometimes steal birds' eggs and young chicks.

17. **Follow the path, passing a bridge on the left. (This leads deeper into the woods, where there are further walks, but the paths are not so safe and there is no circular route.) Pass the bridge and continue through an area of tall conifers. Bear left uphill, partially stepped.**

☺   At the top of the hill, notice, on the left, a view across a farmed field to a group of trees of varying colours. Many are from other countries and were planted by Greg's son, Robert. They are at their best in late Spring and Summer.

18. **Follow the path around a tight bend, through bushes and trees, passing, on the right, several redwoods with soft, flaking bark.**

☺   These trees are called Redwoods, because of the reddish colour of their bark. They grow very tall, and in America some have grown so big that holes have been made in their trunks for cars to drive through.

19. **The path soon bears downhill, zigzagging to a stone bridge.**

☺   This is Chapel Bridge, built by Robert Greg. These woods were originally the grounds of his house, Norcliffe Hall. The small bridge further along the gully is a folly; an attractive showpiece. It is not safe to cross.

20. **Go over Chapel Bridge and climb the steps leading uphill. Bear left up a further set of steps and then left onto the main path. In a short distance you should pass, on the right, a further bridge.**

☺ This is the Centenary Bridge, built to celebrate the 100th anniversary of the National Trust, which owns and maintains this land and many other sites throughout Britain. It was opened on 26 July 1995.

21. **Continue along the path, leaving the woods (passing an information board and map on the right). Continue alongside Norcliffe Chapel.**

☺ The chapel is built of brick with a stone roof. Look at the small belltower where you may be able to see the bell which called the villagers to church on Sunday mornings.

22. **Continue to the centre of the village and take the cobbled driveway opposite the cross, leading, between lawns, towards Estate Cottages.**

☺ These are further houses built by Greg for his workers, and are called "Oak Cottages". About eight people lived in each cottage, very cramped by today's standards, but luxurious compared to the terrible conditions in the Manchester slums. Each of the cottages had a small garden or allotment, so that flowers and vegetables could be grown.

The building at the end of the row **(TO THE LEFT)** is Oak School which Greg built to educate his staff. Younger children came here during the day, and older children, who worked in the mill, came in the evenings or at week-ends. There were also classes for adults, as not all grown-ups could read and write.

(Between the two rows of cottages, on the right, is a shop front with displays of old tins and food packages in its windows.)

☺ This was the village shop, where the mill workers could

Oak Cottages

buy their food; the cost was deducted from their wages. The old tins and packets are very different from modern ones. Are there any you can recognise?

23. **Continue along the path in front of the cottages, passing the allotments on the right, then bear right into the car park.**

Styal Woods & Quarry Bank Mill checklist

- [ ] A BLACK AND WHITE COW
- [ ] A CHURCH SPIRE
- [ ] A SQUIRREL
- [ ] A FIRCONE
- [ ] A PLANE IN FLIGHT
- [ ] A WILD RABBIT
- [ ] IVY ON A TREE OR WALL
- [ ] A DUCK ON WATER
- [ ] A WOODEN BRIDGE
- [ ] A SACK OF SUGAR
- [ ] A TALL MILL CHIMNEY
- [ ] A RED CAR

Swettenham

Swettenham is a pleasant, sleepy village in an unspoiled and very rural area. It is rich, fertile farming country, and fields of corn and wheat are plentiful: the very essence of Cheshire. It is an area renowned for its wildlife along the banks of the River Dane and the Swettenham Brook valley. The ideal place to get away from it all. Apart from the occasional piece of farm machinery, it could be a century ago.

Starting point:	The Swettenham Arms, Swettenham (SJ799672). The village is signed from the A535 Holmes Chapel to Chelford road, and A34 Congleton to Alderley Edge road and is situated just north of the River Dane. The pub is signed in the village, and is easy to find. It is situated directly behind the church. There are a few places around the lanes where parking is available for single cars. Please park sensibly and respect other road users and the villagers. There is parking at the Swettenham Arms for patrons only.
	For a much longer route; ample parking and public toilets can be found at Brereton Heath Park, just south of the A54 Congleton to Holmes Chapel road. From here it is a pleasant walk of 1½ miles to Swettenham. Bear right from the car park, cross the main road and take the bridleway opposite, leading past Davenport Hall. The path crosses the River Dane and leads up to the village.
By train:	Nearest stations; Holmes Chapel and Goostrey. Both have a series of footpaths which can be used to reach Swettenham without using roads.
Distance:	Entire circular route from Swettenham Arms – 3 miles.
Terrain:	Except for a brief climb after crossing Swettenham Brook, the route is entirely flat, using mainly footpaths along fields and farm trackways.
Maps:	OS Landranger 118.
Public Toilets:	Nearest public toilets are at Brereton Heath Park, as mentioned above. There are toilets at the Swettenham Arms for patrons only.
Refreshments:	Swettenham Arms. Tables outside.
Pushchairs:	Although the flat land would be ideal, the number of stiles makes the route impassable to pushchairs. Good flat paths can be found at the Brereton Heath Park.

The Swettenham Arms is a picturesque building of whitewashed brick. It has colourful hanging baskets and window boxes, and seats outside looking towards the church.

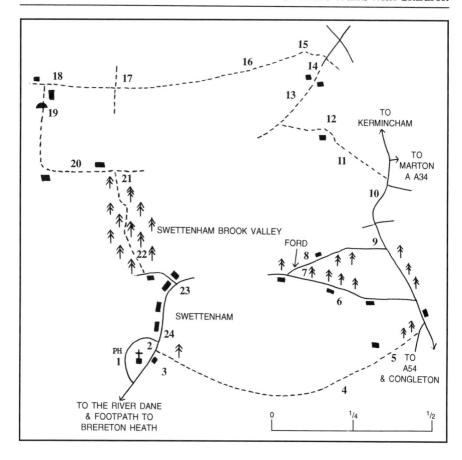

Q: What hangs over the door of the village pub?

A: A lamp or lantern which bears the pub's name: "Swettenham Arms".

1.   From the pub, head for the church and enter the churchyard through the back gate.

☺ This is the church of St Peter. The original wooden spire began to decay and, several hundred years ago, it was surrounded by the present brick tower. The main church building was altered and extended over the years and has many unusual features, like the different shaped windows on the far side and the many "Gargoyles" or stone faces.

The Church at Swettenham

Q: Which animal can you find above one of the doors?

A: Over the side door is a horse's head in a gold crown.

☺ There are many yew trees around the small graveyard. They have thin, dark green leaves and sometimes red berries. Can you recognise them? They can often be found in graveyards because their wood was used for making coffins. Yews can live for thousands of years.

Q: How many stone crosses can you see on the church roof?

A: Two, both on the southern side.

2. **Leave the churchyard by the small gate at the back of the church. Cross over the lane and take the footpath almost opposite. Follow the path through the grounds of a bungalow and into an open field. Cross the field.**

☺ Shuttlingsloe, a hill in East Cheshire, one of the highest points in the county, can be seen on the horizon. It looks like an upturned pudding basin.

Q: There are often cows in this field. Cows are females, what are the males called?

A: Bulls. Bulls often have horns and are usually much larger and heavier than cows. They are supposed to chase anything red. There is a saying "like a red rag to a bull". In fact, bulls are not attracted to red at all.

3. **Head straight across the field. Pass a large tree on the left (with a direction arrow). There should now be a hedge on your left. Continue ahead to a stile.**

☺ Between the trees, **(AHEAD ON THE RIGHT)** you may be able to see a Cheshire landmark on the distant horizon; the castle of Mow Cop. It is actually a mock castle, just a tower and an archway, and was built as an attractive summerhouse. It can be seen from many places around the county.

4. **Climb the stile and continue ahead, passing a farmhouse on the left.**

☺ There may be crops growing in these fields. Grains, such as wheat or corn, or vegetables, especially potatoes. The farmer usually puts a different crop in each field every year, because each crop takes different nutrients out of the soil, and puts other nutrients back. If there is wheat in the field it may be planted with potatoes next year, and corn the year after, or it may be left to grass. Try to recognise any crops you see.

5. **Climb the next stile and continue straight across the field to a stile, then bear left, onto the drive of Swettenham Hall, and left again onto the lane.**

☺ This is the drive to Swettenham Hall, which once was the home of the rich lords who owned most of the area. They would rent farms and cottages to local people, who would grow crops to support themselves.

6. **Pass the houses on the lane. After the old barn on the left, take the right turning, leading downhill.**

*Escape Route:*For the village centre or to return to the starting point do not turn off the lane, continue ahead.

7. **Follow the lane downhill, beneath overhanging trees, to Swettenham Brook.**

☺ This is Swettenham Brook. Where the road goes through the stream it is known as a "ford". There is a depth indicator to show if the water is too deep to drive through. How deep is the water today?

8. **Cross the footbridge and follow the lane uphill.**

Q: What is the name of the first farm on the left?
A: "Brookhouse Farm".

9. **At the top, bear left and follow the lane.**

Q: What is the name of the village you are now entering?

A: Kermincham; there is a boundary sign on the left.

Q: Notice the signpost on the right. How far is Swettenham Heath?

A: Three quarters of a mile.

10. Take the footpath on the left through the hawthorn hedge.

☺ There may be cows in this field or you may see rabbits running for cover as you approach, as there are many rabbit holes, or "burrows" hidden in the hedgerows.

11. Pass behind the stables then bear right over the stile and across the field towards the front of the house.

Q: Which circular objects are on the front of the house and the barn?

A: Cart Wheels.

Q: Next to the house is an old barn. On the roof is a weather vane which shows which way the wind is blowing. What type of animal is on the weather vane?

A: A horse.

12. Continue past the barn to a further stile and bear left along the edge of the field. Climb the stile and bear right along the driveway.

Escape Route: Bear left along the driveway and follow it for $\frac{1}{2}$ mile, then bear left through a five-barred gate into an area of woodland, and continue from direction 21.

☺ There are hedgerows on both sides of the drive, with hawthorn bushes, blackberries, ferns and grasses and many other plants. Hedgerows are very attractive and are usually colourful in every season. They give shelter for birds and small animals, and the red berries on hawthorn and holly bushes provide food through the cold Winter months. Do not eat any wild berries. Animals eat them, but they could poison you.

13. Pass "Cross Lane Cottage" on the right, then "Cross Lane Farm" on the left.

Q: What are the animals on the plaque at the gates to "Cross Lane Farm"?

A: An owl and a hedgehog.

14. A short way after the farm go through the metal gate on the left and along the footpath.

☺ On the left there is a bath for cows to drink from. On the right you should be able to see houses in Kermincham.

15. **Take the stile on the left and continue along the edge of the field to two further stiles.**

☺ From here there are views for miles across the vast Cheshire Plain.

16. **Follow the footpath across a series of stiles, keeping to the right of the fields.**

☺ In some places there are hawthorn hedgerows along the edges of the fields, and in others just barbed wire fences. Many country hedgerows are hundreds of years old and were planted when England was a farming country, with each farmer having just a few fields. Today there are fewer, usually larger, farms.

"Conservationists" are people who want to protect the countryside and keep it safe for us all to enjoy. They encourage farmers not to remove hedges and trees. Do you prefer hedgerows or wire fences?
You may see horses grazing in the fields nearby. Can you recognize any crops that are growing?

Escape Route: After about half a mile, you should pass a stile on the right. This point is a crossroads of footpaths. There is no sign to indicate it, but there is a path leading off to the left, along the edge of the field. For a short cut to Swettenham village, follow the path which drops down to a rutted trackway. Bear right for a short way, then, at the farm buildings, go through a five-barred gate on the left into an area of woodland. Continue from direction 21.

17. **Continuing straight ahead, cross the stile and follow the old brick wall on the right towards a group of farm buildings.**

☺ Look at the old brick wall beside you. The cement is flaking, making some of the bricks loose. Can you see the yellow, green and white growths on the surface of the brick? This is called **LICHEN** and is a type of moss. Lichen needs very little water to survive. In hot weather it dries out, but will be restored by rain.

To the right the huge dish of the Jodrell Bank Radio Telescope can be seen. This is used to pick up signals from space.

18. **Pass the stable and continue to the stile. Keep straight ahead, passing the farm buildings, and go through the five-barred gate onto a driveway.**

Q: Which animal is on the weathervane on the barn roof?
A: A cockerel, which is a male hen.

☺ The house ahead in the distance is Kermincham Hall. It is built of brick and has stone roof slabs. As at Swettenham Hall, the owners would have had land in the area which they rented out.

Q: How many chimney pots can you count on the roof of the hall?

A: Nine.

19. **Bear left along the driveway, passing the back of the barns.**

☺ There may be tractors and other farm machines in these open barns. There are machines to plough fields, plant seeds, cut grass and even dig up potatoes. Once, all these jobs would have been done by hand.

20. **Follow the drive between further farm buildings and continue along the footpath ahead. At the next farm bear right through a five-barred gate.**

☺ Look for squirrels running along the branches. At one time there were more red squirrels than grey, but now there are very few. Red squirrels find it more difficult to find food, while the grey squirrels are mischievous and very clever, and will raid bird tables and litter bins. If you see a squirrel it will almost certainly be a grey one.

21. **Follow the track downhill through the trees and cross the stream.**

☺ **(AT THE BRIDGE)** This is Swettenham Brook. The trees in the meadows surrounding the brook are mainly alders. There is a great deal of wildlife here, particularly birds, including kingfishers and woodpeckers.

22. **After the bridge, the track leads uphill. Bear left at the top.**

Q: Some of the windows of the cottage on the right have been bricked up. How many?

A: Three on this side, and one on the front above the door.

23. **Bear right onto the lane to the centre of the village.**

Q: What type of flower is the cottage on the right named after? (It has a round window upstairs and a face over the door.)

A: A White Rose. ("White Rose Cottage").

24. **Bear right at the war memorial before the church and back to the Swettenham Arms.**

Other Places of Interest in the Area

Daffodil Dell
Through the nursery at Swettenham. There is a small car park next to the brook.

Swettenham checklist

☐ A CHURCH TOWER

☐ A HANGING LAMP

☐ A BLACK AND WHITE COW

☐ A HORSE

☐ A WHITE COTTAGE

☐ A TRACTOR

☐ A WOODEN BRIDGE

☐ A BRICK OR STONE BRIDGE

☐ A RABBIT'S BURROW

☐ AN OLD BATH

☐ A TELEPHONE BOX

☐ A POST BOX

Tatton Park

Tatton park has something for all of the family. Impressive landscape, formal gardens, and two historic halls in a setting with a rich ancient and medieval past. Of special interest to children: paddling and swimming are permitted in the lake. There is a bathing enclosure on the eastern bank and a safe area marked by buoys. Close to the hall there is a good children's playground. The park is famous for its red and fallow deer, and a host of other creatures, wild and domesticated, can often be seen.

Starting point:	Knutsford Gates (SJ752792). There is a car park immediately on the right. The walk works equally well from the main car park, close to the hall. (SJ742817).
By rail:	Nearest station: Knutsford. A short walk through the town centre to the Knutsford gates of the park. Well-signposted.
Distance:	4 miles.
Terrain:	Flat parkland, suitable for all weather.
Maps:	OS Landrangers 109 & 118 (both needed to cover entire park).
Public Toilets:	Mere Car Park
	Stableyard, near hall
Refreshments:	Stables Restaurant, near hall
	Tuck Shop near hall
Pushchairs:	The flat park is ideal for pushchairs. The paths used are not concrete, so they are uneven, but easily negotiable.

1. **From the Knutsford entrance, bear left from the drive, along the avenue of beech trees.**

☺ The park is now open to the public, but it was once private and belonged to the Lord of Tatton Manor. The Egertons, the family owning the manor, were very wealthy and powerful. The last Lord Egerton had no relatives, so he left it to the National Trust. They look after the park and house and open it to the public.

These trees did not grow naturally in neat rows. The whole park has been carefully laid out, and in many places trees have been planted to form "avenues".

2. **Continue along the beech avenue, passing a golf course on the left.**

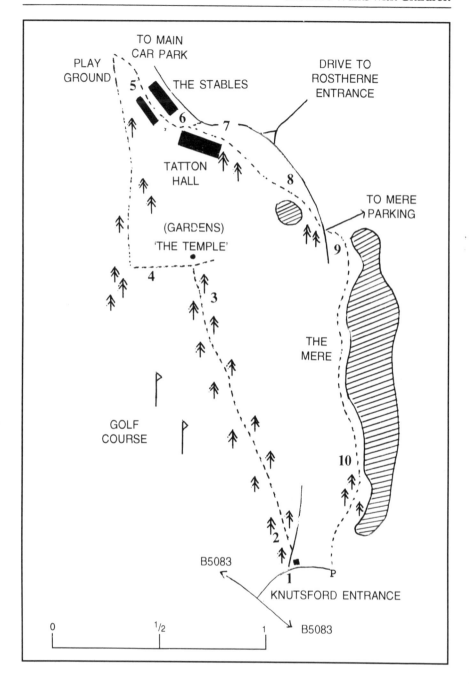

Fallow Deer

☺ The park has many deer which can often be seen sheltering beneath the trees. Here there are two different types of deer. Fallow deer are smaller and have white spots on their coats. Red deer are larger and have reddish brown coats.

Q: What do you think deer eat?

A: Leaves and young shoots mainly, but also the bark of young trees.

You may see rabbits along the avenue. They live in holes in the ground called "burrows". You may see some burrows between the roots of trees. Notice how the soil is very sandy as much of Cheshire is on sandstone.
(TOWARDS THE END OF THE AVENUE) Some trees have fallen or been blown over, and others have been cut down or "felled" for safety, so new trees have been planted to replace them.

3.   **Continue ahead, towards "The Temple" (a folly monument in the hall gardens). At the end of the path bear left and climb the stile, heading for the far right corner of the field.**

Pushchair route: Bear right at "The Temple" and follow the path, keeping left, which will take you to the hall, restaurant and toilets. For the return journey follow direction 5 & onwards.

☺ There are often sheep grazing in this field. Look for strands of wool in the grass, and keep a look out for any deer or squirrels.

4. Climb the further stile and follow the trackway through the trees. When the track bears away to the left, keep straight ahead across open parkland, heading towards the children's playground. Go through the gate to the left of the playground and bear right. Keep right, bearing along a pathway through the trees which leads to the stableyard, restaurant and toilets.

☺ **(IN THE COBBLED STABLEYARD)** The restaurant, with the clocktower, was once the stable block for up to fifty horses.

(IN THE SHEDS OPPOSITE THE RESTAURANT) Here you can see Tatton's horse-drawn fire engine, with a row of firemens' helmets along its side. When it was in use, it would have raced to put out any fire in the hall or the grounds.

Q: What colour is the fire engine?

A: Red.

5. Continue through the stableyard, passing the tuck shop on the left. Cross the cobbled driveway and take the path opposite, through the trees.

Those wishing to visit the hall should continue ahead along the cobbled drive. Hall opening times may vary due to special events

6. Go through the double iron gates and bear right, passing the front of the house.

☺ This was the main entrance to the hall. There are views from the windows along the avenue of trees and over the parkland.

7. Continue past the hall, following a path through the trees. When the path splits, bear left across the parkland. The path soon becomes difficult to see, but continue ahead, keeping roughly parallel to the Knutsford Drive, on your left.

The Hall from the Gardens

☺ You may notice many planes passing overhead, usually one every few minutes. If you watch them carefully you can see them landing at Manchester Airport. **(LARGE WHITE BUILDINGS, JUST VISIBLE TO THE LEFT, OVER THE CHESHIRE PLAIN.)**

During the war, Tatton Park was used for training parachutists. They could land safely in the open spaces in the park.

Look for the deer. In hot weather they like to be in the shade beneath the trees.

8. **Pass Melchett Mere on the right and continue a short way along the drive. Pass the turning to the left and, immediately after, bear diagonally across the grass to the head of the lake.**

☺ Tatton Mere is not a natural lake. It was made when the Monks from nearby Mobberley built a dam across a river, so flooding the valley.

The head of the mere is sheltered so birds can swim in safety. There are often swans and ducks, and Canada Geese with black and white heads.

9. **Bear right along the edge of the mere. Climb the stile and continue close to the water.**

Those with pushchairs may find it easier to continue along the Knutsford Drive

Route B: For an alternative route back to Knutsford, bear left and keep close to the water's edge. On the other side of the lake, pass the bathers' enclosure and continue through woodland to the large wooden park gate. Go through this and follow the driveway through the woods, bearing right at the end for the town centre.

☺ In fine weather there are often boats and windsurfers on the water, and sometimes people swimming. When it is very hot, cows wade a short way into the lake to drink and keep cool.

(TOWARDS THE END OF THE LAKE YOU SHOULD PASS AN AREA OF TREES ON THE RIGHT.) There are many squirrels in the woods around Tatton. They eat nuts and seeds and can often be seen running along branches or rummaging on the ground, looking for food.

10. **Follow the path as it bears away from the lake and leads uphill to the Knutsford car park and gates.**

Tatton Park checklist

☐ A CHURCH TOWER

☐ A PLANE IN FLIGHT

☐ A SWAN

☐ A CANADA GOOSE

☐ A SQUIRREL

☐ A WHITE CAR

☐ A RABBIT

☐ AN OLD FIRE ENGINE

☐ A FALLOW DEER (Small, with white spots on coat)

☐ A RED DEER (Larger, with a reddish brown coat)

𝒲𝒽𝒶𝓇𝓉𝑜𝓃'𝓈 𝓛𝑜𝒸𝓀 & 𝓉𝒽𝑒 𝓢𝒽𝓇𝑜𝓅𝓈𝒽𝒾𝓇𝑒 𝒰𝓃𝒾𝑜𝓃 𝒞𝒶𝓃𝒶𝓁

The Shropshire Union Canal runs through this picturesque area near to Tiverton, providing a great deal of interest for children and adults. The magnificent ruin of Beeston Castle, high on its rocky crag, adds to the splendid scenery.

This walk was originally intended as part of a much longer route, which had to be abandoned due to footpath problems (i.e. they were blocked, kept disappearing, were unsigned, badly stiled etc.). Nevertheless, this short circuit has been retained, because this stretch of the canal is so spectacular. It is an ideal stroll for a warm Summer's evening, before visiting the "Shady Oak" pub which overlooks the canal. (There are seats outside and a children's playground.)

Starting point:	Bate's Mill Lane, near the Shady Oak Pub. (SJ533603). There is parking at the Shady Oak for patrons and some places along the lane, where the verge allows. To find "The Shady Oak", turn off into Tiverton Village from the A49, just below Tarporley. Follow the road and take the first left, signed for Beeston Castle. The pub is ½ mile on the left.
Distance:	Just under 2 miles.
Terrain:	Almost entirely flat; canal towpaths, public footpaths, and some lanes.
Maps:	OS Landranger 117
Public Toilets:	No public toilets in the area. Toilets in "The Shady Oak" for patrons only. Nearest public toilets on main street, Tarporley.
Refreshments:	"The Shady Oak"
Pushchairs:	The canal path is easily accessible for pushchairs. Walk from "The Shady Oak", along the towpath to Wharton's Lock, then return the same way.

1.   **From "The Shady Oak", cross the canal bridge and bear left, through the gate onto the towpath.**

☺ Canals are not rivers. They are man-made; dug out of the earth and filled with water. Many were built to carry goods, such as coal or, in the case of Cheshire, salt from mines to factories. These goods are now carried by road or rail, and canals are used mainly for pleasure. You will probably see several canal houseboats along this stretch. These are called "narrow boats" and are often brightly painted and decorated with pictures of flowers. Some even have real flowers, in hanging baskets or in tubs on the roof. Many have names such as "Nutcracker" or "Shropshire Queen." Can you see any with names?

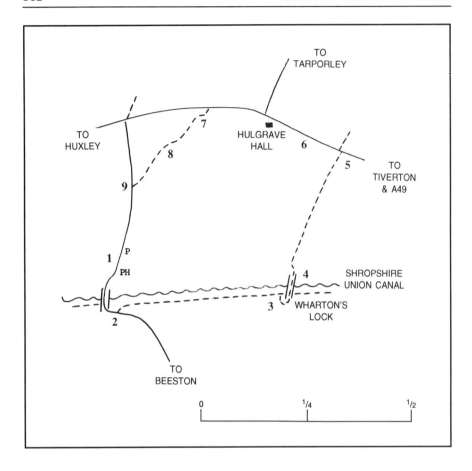

Q: What number is on the bridge near "The Shady Oak"?

A: 109.

2. Bear right along the towpath.

😊 **(ON THE RIGHT)** The castle, which can be seen for miles, is Beeston Castle. The site has been used for defence for thousands of years, but the present castle was built in 1220 by the Earl of Chester. It has been damaged in wars and is now in ruins, but still looks very impressive.

There are many plants along the edge of the water, including reeds, rushes, thistles and nettles. Have you noticed that the water is a sandy brown colour?

The Shropshire Union Canal, near The Shady Oak

This is because, when the canal was dug, the sides and bottom were covered with a thick clay to make them water-tight. The clay has coloured the water.

This is a popular place for canal boats to stop overnight, mainly because of the pub. People can meet each other and exchange boating stories. It is also a popular place for swans and ducks, because they are likely to be given food. Swans, once they find a mate, stay together for life and protect their young, or "cygnets", until they are nearly fully grown. Don't go too close as the swans can be dangerous.

3. **Pass under the bridge, go up the steps and cross the canal by the footbridge. Take care, this water is deep!**

☺ This is Wharton's Lock. A "lock" is used as a kind of lift, to raise or lower canal boats. The level of the water on one side is much higher than the other. If you are lucky, you may see a boat using the lock, so you can watch how it works.

(The best chance of seeing the lock in use is at the week-end. There is a picnic site on the opposite side of the canal, close to the lock.)

4. **Take the stile near the bridge and bear left. Keep to the path alongside the edge of the field.**

☺ The hedgerow on the left is made up of many different plants and trees, including hawthorn (with sharp thorns and bright red berries in the Autumn and Winter), sloe (with sharp thorns and purple berries in the Autumn) and oaks.

A thick hedgerow is popular, as a shelter, with birds and small animals so look and listen.

The field on your right may have cows in it, but is often used for crops, such as wheat, which is a grass-like crop, or corn, which is very tall and green, and produces sweet corn on "cobs" which you may recognise.

5. **Cross the stile onto the lane and bear left. There is a narrow grass verge along the edge of the road.**

☺ Again there are views of the castle, over the hedges on the left. There is an old legend that King Richard II hid his treasure in the castle and that it is still there. It is believed that if the treasure really exists, it must be at the bottom of the deep well.

6. **Pass Hulgrave Hall on the left, then go through the next metal gate on the left. (At the time of writing, this public footpath is unsigned.)**

(Alternatively, continue along the lane, taking the first left turning back to "The Shady Oak".)

7. **Bear right to a gate next to a water trough. Go through this and bear diagonally right across the field, passing the pond.**

☺ Reeds and bulrushes grow in and around this pond. There are often cows here which leave hoofprints in the mud around the pond when they come to drink.

Cows are curious and may approach you, but will usually shy away if you make any sudden moves. Never walk closely behind a large animal. If startled, they may kick out at you with their back legs.

8. **Continue across the field and go through the metal gate in the middle of the far fence. Bear diagonally right to another metal gate which opens onto the lane.**

Q: What is the name for a young cow?

A: A calf.

☺ If cows are lying down it supposedly means it is going to rain, but cows, like weathermen, can make mistakes.

9. **Bear left and continue back to "The Shady Oak".**

☺ Sheltering in the undergrowth along the lane, there may be rabbits, hedgehogs or field mice. There are often holes made by badgers in the sandy soil. The sand is piled up outside the entrance. Badgers only come out at night, so you are unlikely to see one. Sometimes foxes live in old badger holes.

The hedges are mainly hawthorn and the trees along the lane are mainly oaks, which produce acorns. In the Autumn you will probably see acorns on the lane.

Q: What is the name of the pub next to the canal?

A: "The Shady Oak". On the sign there is a picture of a large oak tree, with cool shade beneath its branches.

(The walk is over. Children to the play area. Adults to the bar.)

Other Places of Interest

Beeston Castle

From "The Shady Oak" continue across the canal and follow the lane around to the left. The castle is well-signed. Open daily from April to October, 10am to 6pm. A short climb up Beeston crag to the castle, from which there are unspoiled panoramic views in all directions. There is a museum depicting the history of the castle and its role in the civil war.

Wharton's Lock checklist

☐ A CANAL BOAT

☐ A SWAN

☐ A BRICK BRIDGE

☐ A CASTLE

☐ A COW

☐ A TRACTOR

☐ A BLUE CAR

☐ A BLACK & WHITE HOUSE

☐ A RABBIT

☐ A HANGING PUB SIGN

☐ A DOG

☐ IVY

𝒯he 𝒲hitegate 𝒲ay and 𝒱ale 𝒭oyal

The Whitegate Way is a permitted footpath along an old railway line, passing through Vale Royal, and some of Cheshire's most attractive countryside. Relatively flat with many views over the patchwork fields towards the Peckforton Hills.

Starting point:	Whitegate Way Car Park at the old station (SJ615679) well-signed from A556 and A54 in the Vale Royal district.
By rail:	Nearest station: Cuddington, but there is a connecting bus service from Delamere station.
By bus:	Services from Northwich, Middlewich, Delamere station and Winsford.
Distance:	Entire route: 5 miles, with many escape routes.
Terrain:	Half of the route is along the Whitegate Way, an old railway track, now an attractive footpath. Paths across farmed fields and trackways. All relatively flat.
Maps:	OS Landranger 118
Public Toilets:	Towards the end of the car park.
Refreshments:	Nowhere along the route, but try the cafe at Jardinerie Garden Centre, Cotebrook, or the Craft Centre on the A556 at Sandiway.
Pushchairs:	The Whitegate Way is ideal for pushchairs. The rest of the route, however, crosses farmland and is unsuitable. From the car park it is possible to walk for several miles in each direction along the old railway. Return the same way.

☺ **(AT WHITEGATE STATION)** This was once a railway station. As you can see from the large concrete sign it was called "Whitegate" Station, after the nearby village. The house was once the ticket office and waiting room. It is now a private home. There is an old trolley outside the house which would have been used to carry suitcases.

1. **Bear right along the narrow track.**

☺ Steam trains would once have rattled along here. The railway was opened in 1870 to carry salt from the mines at Winsford to Cuddington, 6 miles away, where the salt could be loaded onto the main railway line that ran (and still runs) between Chester and Manchester.

There are many silver birch trees, with narrow white trunks, growing along the track. There are also nettles and brambles growing on the banks, so take care.

2. **Pass the toilet block on the right and go through the gate. Continue ahead.**

☺ Amongst the other trees along the track there is a pear tree, on the left. In the Summer you should be able to see the fruit.

The path is also used by horses, so look for hoofprints on the ground.
The railway was used for 82 years, finally closing in 1952. In 1970 the metal tracks were lifted and taken away to be re-used. When metal is heated sufficiently, it turns into a liquid which can be made into new objects.

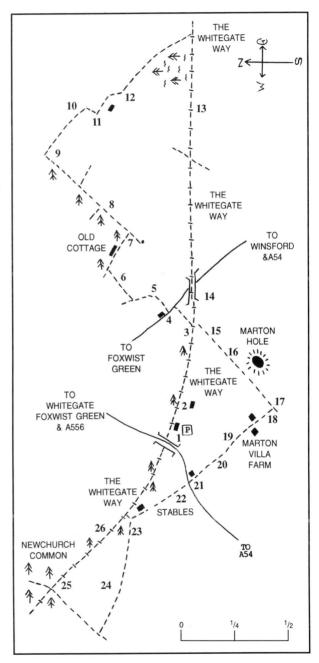

3. **Avoid the first footpath to the left, but take the second one, leading down a set of steps, signed "Marton Sands". Continue to the lane.**

☺ In the field on the right there are usually black and white cows which are called "friesians". Most of the cows in Cheshire are black and white Friesians.

4. **Carefully cross the lane and take the stile almost opposite, signed "Beauty Bank". Follow the narrow path through the undergrowth to a stile. Keep left along the edge of the field.**

☺ On the steep bank on the left there are many wild plants, which you may recognise. Gorse is a bush with very sharp prickles and yellow flowers for most of the year. Rosebay willow herb is a common plant along hedgerows and on wasteland in towns. It is tall, with pink flowers throughout the Spring and Summer.

5. **Follow the path as it begins to climb slightly and bears around to the left. At this point bear right and cross the field to the stile in the fence.**

☺ Look back towards the railway line, and notice how it runs along a bank which has been built across the countryside. This is called an "embankment". Have you ever noticed that a train journey is always flat? Trains can't go uphill or downhill, so the tracks are flat and embankments like this have to be built, or "cuttings" are made through higher ground. Trains also go over bridges and through tunnels, to keep the tracks level. You can see two bridges from here, one over the road, the other over a farm driveway.

6. **Continue straight ahead, across the field, to the hedgerow opposite, then bear right, keeping to the edge of the field. A path leads downhill to a stile in the hedge. Climb this and follow the footpath.**

☺ Near the stile there is a damson tree. In the Summer it will be covered with dark purple fruit. Damsons are a type of plum and can be made into jam or wine.

You will soon pass a row of brick cottages, with old square windows and arched doorways. After the cottages the path goes downhill between overhanging trees.

7. **Join the trackway at the bottom, bearing left over the cattle grid.**

☺ In the woods on the left there is a stream flowing between the trees. On the right is a high bank covered with ivy and bracken. Bracken is a type of fern, with feather-like leaves. Ivy is a climbing plant. Notice how it winds its way around the bark of the trees.

8. **Avoid the first footpath to the left and continue ahead along the track. The**

track soon bears sharply to the right. On the corner, take the footpath that leads straight ahead along the stream.

☺ Willows like moisture so can often be found close to streams and ponds, as here. There are also several tall oak trees.

Q: What is the fruit of the oak tree called?

A: An acorn. The fruit of a plant contains the seeds. If you plant an acorn it will grow into an oak tree. Apples are fruit because they contain pips which are the seeds of the apple tree.

9. At the end of the field take the stile and bear right, with a hedge on your right.

☺ The pond below is private. There are often Highland cattle in the fields in this area. They came originally from Scotland and have long horns and long shaggy coats which would have kept them warm through the long Scottish winters.

Highland cattle near The Whitegate Way

10. Cross the next stile and bear right along a gravel trackway towards the whitewashed house.

11. After a short way, bear left across the stile, passing in front of the house. Continue ahead, crossing a number of stiles in close succession, until you come to a large open field. Here, bear right, keeping close to the hedge.

☺ This very large field would once have been several smaller fields, surrounded by hedges and trees. Farmers have removed the hedges to enable them to use modern farming machines. Can you tell which crop is growing in the field?

12. **At the end of the hedge keep straight ahead, cutting across the field towards the area of trees. Keep the trees on your right and continue to the stile. This leads back to the Whitegate Way. Bear right.**

☺ You return to the old railway. Look back over the countryside you have just crossed. The track soon leads between bracken and overhanging trees. Banks on both sides of the track show that this is a "cutting". Can you remember that a "cutting" is a channel cut through the ground, to make way for the railway?

13. **Ignore stiles on either side, and continue, as the track crosses a road.**

☺ The railway is built on an "embankment" so it is higher than the surrounding countryside. This gives views over the first part of the walk.

14. **The track crosses a driveway. Shortly afterwards, go down the steps on the left to the stile, signed "Marton Hole/Chester Lane".**

*Escape Route:*To return to the starting point, continue ahead along the old railway.

15. **Climb the stile and proceed across the middle of the field.**

☺ There may be cows or crops in these fields. You should soon come to a pond, with steep sides leading down to very deep water. This is Marton Hole which appeared overnight when the land fell into a hole left by salt mining. There are sometimes ducks or black coots on the water.

16. **Pass the hole on the left and continue ahead to the hedge, then bear left along the edge of a field, towards the telegraph poles.**

☺ Here are views over the Cheshire Plain to the Peckforton Hills, where there is a castle built amongst the trees.

17. **Take the stile to the right in the hedge, and continue towards the farm buildings.**

18. **Follow a series of stiles and enter the farmyard by a gate. Continue along the driveway.**

☺ This is "Marton Villa Farm". Further along the driveway is a small, reedy pond. In the Summer there are water lilies with round, rubbery leaves and red flowers. They grow in the mud at the bottom of the pond, and the leaves and flowers grow to the surface on long stems. The flowers close at night and in poor weather.

19. **Cross the cattle grid, passing a small cottage on the left.**

☺ On the left is a small cottage with roses growing on its walls. The bottom half of the cottage is made of local sandstone, and the top half is brick.

20. Keep right along the driveway.

Q: Soon you will pass a bungalow on the right. A bungalow is a house which is all on ground level. What is the name of the bungalow?

A: "Calderstone".

21. Cross the lane and follow the trackway.

Escape Route: Bear right and follow the lane a short distance back to Whitegate station, on the right.

22. Continue along the trackway, passing the stables on the right.

☺ There are stables on the right, so you are likely to see horses, either at the stables, or along this trackway, which is used as a "bridleway"; or path for horses.

Escape Route: Take the footpath, to the right after the stables, which leads to the Whitegate Way. Bear right along the old railway to the station car park, following direction 25.

23. Continue ahead.

☺ On the left is "Common Farm", and on the right is a field that is sometimes used as a caravan site. Along the track there are blackberry plants with their long, prickly stems. The plant flowers in the Spring, and in the Summer has small berries which ripen from green to black.

24. Bear right along the footpath between fields.

☺ On both sides of the path are fields which often have cows in them. There are several old baths for the cows to drink from. A cow can drink 120 pints of water a day, approximately a bathful.

You should soon reach the old railway again. Here the old rails were left in place to stop this busy part of the path becoming muddy. The metal rails are laid on thick planks of wood which are called "sleepers".

25. Bear right along the line.

☺ There are many rabbits, so look for burrows in the banks along the track. The trees are popular with small birds, such as sparrows and robins. There are more blackberry bushes, nettles and wild flowers which attract insects such as butterflies and dragonflies.

Soon you should pass under a road bridge. The increase in traffic has meant that wooden supports have had to be installed to cope with the extra load.

26. Pass under the bridge and continue ahead to the car park.

☺ Ahead is the old station building which you passed at the start of the walk. The high wall on the right was once the platform. One of the downstairs windows of the house is circular as it once held the station clock.

Vale Royal & Whitegate checklist

- ☐ A CHURCH STEEPLE
- ☐ A RABBIT HOLE
- ☐ A BLACK AND WHITE COW
- ☐ A HORSE
- ☐ IVY GROWING ON A TREE
- ☐ A POND
- ☐ A PICNIC TABLE
- ☐ A BLACKBERRY BUSH
- ☐ A WATER LILY
- ☐ A WHITE HOUSE
- ☐ A DOG
- ☐ METAL TRAIN TRACK

Wincle

Wincle is on the south-eastern edge of the county. The River Dane, just along the lane, marks the boundary between Cheshire and Staffordshire. This is excellent hilly walking country, but quiet and unspoiled. The walk is short, and, if taken at a leisurely pace, makes an enjoyable and varied excursion, with some fine views into Staffordshire.

Starting point:	Wincle (off the A54 Congleton to Buxton road) (SJ964652). Parking available on the left of the road towards Danebridge.
Distance:	Entire route 2 miles. To avoid the brief, steep stretch at the beginning, park as close to "The Ship Inn" as possible and take the footpath just after the inn. Keep straight ahead, then follow Direction 4 and onwards.
Terrain:	Good paths for most of the way. Uphill or flat on the way out, a pleasant downhill stroll to return.
Maps:	OS Landranger 118, OS Outdoor Leisure 24
Refreshments:	"The Ship Inn", Wincle. Beer garden at rear.
Public Toilets:	No public toilets.
Pushchairs:	Not suitable for pushchairs due to the undulating land and many stiles.

1. **Walk down the lane towards Danebridge and take the footpath on the left, almost opposite the telephone box.**

Q: On the post box **(TO THE RIGHT OF THE STILE)** are the letters "ER". What do you think they stand for?

A: They stand for "Elizabeth Regina", which is "Queen Elizabeth" in Latin. This shows that this post box was made during the reign of the present queen. Look at post boxes near your home and see if they have other letters, such as "GR" (for King George) or "VR" (for Queen Victoria).

2. **Follow the steep footpath uphill, to the left, climbing another stile.**

☺ Look at the tree stump. **(TO THE RIGHT, SHORTLY AFTER THE STILE.)** It is flaking away as it rots and will eventually crumble into the soil and feed the other plants.

3. **Continue uphill and climb a further stile under a row of trees.**

☺ These trees are Oaks and their seeds are called acorns. They fall off in Autumn and some of them will grow into new trees. If it is Autumn or Winter, look for them on the ground.

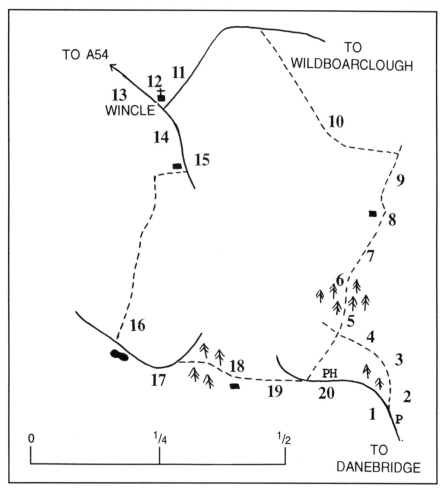

4. Pass behind some houses on the left, and bear right across the open field, towards the signpost in the middle. Continue ahead, bearing downhill to a stile between conifers.

☺ Look for fircones on the ground. The cone carries the seeds of the tree. These seeds are much smaller than acorns and can blow in the wind to take root and grow elsewhere.

5. Follow the path downhill through the woods.

☺ New trees have been planted in the woods. They may have plastic "protectors" around their thin trunks, to stop wild animals from eating their soft bark. The new trees on this side of the stream are mainly rowan, birch and lime. Can you recognise them?

6. **Cross the stream by the stone crossing and continue up the path.**

☺ On this side of the stream there are more young trees, mainly oaks.

7. **Cross the stile and follow the path straight ahead. Soon a farmhouse will come into view on the left. Head towards this.**

☺ **(JUST BEFORE THE STILE INTO THE FARMYARD)** Notice the water troughs for animals to drink from. They are carved from blocks of sandstone and are quite old. There are often cows or sheep in this field.

8. **Climb the stile, and bear to the right along the farm driveway.**

☺ This is "Bartomley Farm", and it, too, is built from sandstone, a local stone which can easily be cut into blocks for building. **(TO THE RIGHT OF THE DRIVEWAY)** This sandstone wall is a different colour because it is weathered and dirty. If you take a close look, you can see that it is made of millions of grains of sand.

9. **Follow the driveway as it swings to the left, leading uphill.**

☺ On the grassy bank by the roadside there are many wild plants, grasses and, in Spring and Summer, many different flowers. How many you can spot?

(Higher up, there are good views to the left, over the Wincle area.)

10. **The driveway soon levels and Wincle church comes into view below. At the end of the driveway bear left along the lane.**

☺ **(ON THE RIGHT, JUST BEFORE THE CHURCH)** This is the local school, and probably smaller than your own school. Children from farms and villages several miles away come here to learn, because it is the only school in the area.

11. **Climb the steps to the church.**

☺ The church has a square bell tower. The bells were rung on Sunday mornings to call people to church. Some of the gravestones are very old. Which is the oldest you can find?

Q: What do you think the metal objects on each side of the church door are used for?

A: They are foot-scrapers, for cleaning dirt from your shoes before going into the church.

12. **Leave the churchyard via the upper gate, to the left of the main entrance.**

🙂 The trees on each side of the gates are yews. You can find them in many old churchyards. People once believed they would keep away evil spirits. The wood was used to make coffins.

13. **Continue past the cottages on the right, then bear left along the lane leading downhill.**

🙂 The cottages **(ON THE RIGHT)** are very old, and are built of local sandstone with heavy stone slabs on the roof.

Q: What is the name of the first cottage after the church?
A: "Little Chapter".

14. **Continue along the lane, passing the church, then leading uphill.**

Q: What is the name of the first farm on the right?
A: "Lane House Farm".

🙂 **(ON THE RIGHT, "THE PARSONAGE")** This big house is "The Parsonage", where the parson or vicar of the church lived.

Escape Route: To return to the starting point, continue ahead along the lane.

15. **Take the footpath on the right directly after the Parsonage. Keep straight ahead, following the edge of the field. After the row of hawthorn trees bear left, cutting diagonally across the field. The stile is just to the right of the telegraph pole. Keep straight ahead, keeping the fence on the left.**

🙂 **(SOME DISTANCE AHEAD THE PATH PASSES A STRANDED STONE GATEPOST.)** The metal hinge shows this was once a gatepost, but the gate, and the wall in which it stood, are now long gone.

16. **Go through the metal gate at the end of the field, and bear left along the lane.**

🙂 There is a pond opposite, surrounded by bulrushes and many different trees.

17. **Go over the cattle-grid and follow the lane. Soon there is a footpath off to the right. Follow this to another stile into woodlands. Follow the path downhill.**

🙂 These tall trees are beeches. In the Autumn you can find beechnuts on the ground. They have prickly shells which split into four to release the seeds. Some of the seeds will begin to grow into new trees, others will be eaten by wild animals, such as squirrels. If you are quiet you may see a squirrel collecting nuts or running along the branches above.

Mother and child, Wincle

18. At the bottom of the woods climb over the stone stile. Take care as it may be slippery on the other side. Continue ahead along the edge of the field, passing a farmhouse on the right. Climb the stile, cross the farm driveway to the opposite stile.

☺ There may be horses in this field. There is a small stable in the **(LEFT)** corner.

19. Cut across the field to another stile and steps that lead down to the lane. Bear right, passing "The Ship Inn". (There is a beer garden at the back of the inn, very pleasant on a sunny day.)

Q: What is painted on the hanging sign over the door of the inn?

A: A ship, of course!

20. Continue along the lane, heading downhill to the parking spaces.

Q: What is the name of the first house on the left after the inn?

A: "Lilac Cottage".

(Take care on the road. Be aware of oncoming traffic.)

Other Places of Interest in the Area

The River Dane, just down the lane in Staffordshire. there are footpaths to the left along its banks.

Wincle checklist

☐ IVY ON A TREE OR GATEPOST

☐ A BLACK AND WHITE COW

☐ AN OLD FASHIONED LAMP POST

☐ A HORSESHOE

☐ A HANGING INN SIGN

☐ A SANDSTONE WALL

☐ A SHEEP

☐ A BIRD'S FEATHER

☐ A GRAVESTONE

☐ A CHIMNEY

Windgather Rocks & Shining Tor

This area is a complete contrast to the more typical flat farmland generally associated with Cheshire. It is wild and rugged in parts, dramatic and stark to some, but most notably, it is usually windy. This walk can conveniently be divided. The southern section has a valley bottom walk through one of the most remote areas of the county. The ascent of Shining Tor is a steady, but quite straightforward, climb to spectacular views. This is the longest walk in the book, but there are various escape routes.

Starting point:	Pym Chair car park (SJ995768) from Macclesfield follow signs for Buxton, then Goyt Valley. Pass Jenkin Chapel on the corner at Saltersford, follow the road uphill, then bear left before the descent into the Goyt Valley. The car park is on the right.
By bus:	Services from Macclesfield to Kettleshulme. From the village head along Side End Lane for a short way and take the first public footpath on the right. Join the route at direction 16
Distance:	Entire route 8 miles, with various escape routes. Northern route only 4½ miles. Southern route only, 4½ miles (bear left from the car park, then right at the junction. Follow the lane downhill for just under ½ mile, then take the footpath on the left. Continue from direction 29)
Terrain:	Moorland paths and farm trackways. Some climbing, especially on southern route
Maps:	OS Landranger 118, OS Outdoor Leisure 24
Public Toilets:	None along the route. The nearest are in the Goyt Valley, across the dam, or the car park & picnic area at Lamaload Reservoir
Refreshments:	Nearest place is the Tea Cosy cafe, on the main road in Kettleshulme, open Friday to Monday. Closed in January.
Pushchairs:	Impossible

1. From the main Pym Chair car park, face the road and bear right across the grass verge at the side of the lane. After a short distance there is a stile on the right. Cross this and bear left along the dry-stone wall.

☺ This is one of the windiest and loneliest parts of Cheshire. You are on the boundary between Cheshire and Derbyshire, and this type of country is more typical of Derbyshire. If you have been on other walks in Cheshire you will know that it is mainly flat with green fields, woodlands and colourful hedgerows. Here the land is higher, and, to your left, you should be able to see over the hills towards the lower parts of the county.

Ahead there are views of the Goyt Forest, in Derbyshire. The trees are mainly conifers, with long, dark green needles instead of leaves. Conifers have very straight trunks and grow fairly quickly, so they are often grown for their wood.

Q: Most conifers are "evergreens". Do you know what an "evergreen" is?

A: It is a tree or bush which does not lose its leaves in the Winter, so it stays green all the year round. Many evergreen trees and bushes are used as decorations at Christmas. These include holly, ivy and Christmas trees.

☺ In the Autumn or Winter, you should

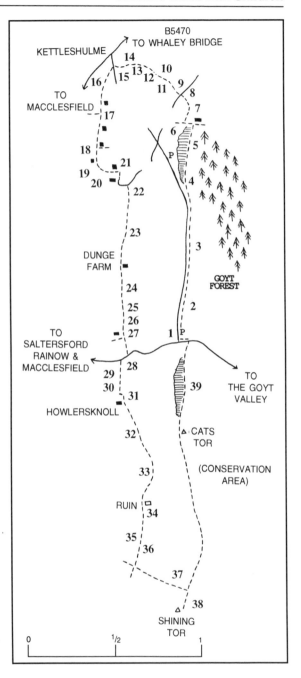

Near Pym Chair

see that some of the conifers have changed colour. They are brown or yellow, and may have started to lose their needles. These trees are "larches" and are grown for their wood. They are obviously not evergreens, but "deciduous".

Q: What does "deciduous" mean?
A: Deciduous trees lose their leaves in the Winter. New leaves will appear in the Spring.

☺ This type of countryside is called "moorland". Apart from the forest, which was planted by man, there are very few trees. There are wild grasses and low bushes, like heather, which grow well in such places, where it can be bitterly cold in the Winter, and very windy, even in Summer. Heather has small, colourful flowers of white, pink, purple or red. It is often used in gardens.

2. **Keep ahead, following the wall. Avoid the stile on the left which leads back to the lane.**

☺ On the right there is a conifer plantation, which is like a small forest. The ground between the trees is covered with dead needles which have fallen from the trees. Evergreens shed their needles gradually, throughout the year, and they are constantly replaced by new ones.

3. **Follow the path and climb the stile soon after the plantation. Continue ahead along the top of Windgather Rocks, taking care of the drop on the left.**

☺ This area is called Windgather Rocks, and you can probably understand why. It is high and often very windy. Don't go too near the "cliff edge", or you may be blown off! The "cliff" is popular with rock climbers, who come to practise here. They can often be seen climbing the rocks at weekends.

4.   **Continue straight ahead, and cross a stone stile in the wall at the end, not the wooden stile on the right leading down into the forest. Keep ahead, with the rocks, and later a dry-stone wall, on your left.**

☺ The Goyt Forest should be below, on your right. The trees are mainly conifers. Sometimes areas of the trees are cleared and the wood is taken to be made into furniture, or "woodpulp", from which paper is made. New trees are then replanted, so there will always be trees here.

5.   **At the end of the field go through a stone gateway onto a gravel track. Bear left, and pass the farmhouse. Continue along the driveway for a short way to the ladder stile on the right.**

Escape Route: Continue to the end of the driveway and keep left, which will return you to the starting point in 1½ miles.

6.   **Climb the ladder stile, passing a small plantation of conifers. Go through the gate and cross the small field to a further gate and stile. Continue straight ahead across an open field.**

☺ There are often sheep or cows in these fields. Sometimes they lie close to the walls, keeping out of the wind, and who can blame them?

7.   **Climb the stile at the far side of the field, and continue downhill towards the houses.**

☺ Ahead you should be able to see the rooftops of the village of Kettleshulme where "candlewick" was made until recent years. This was often used to make bedspreads.

8.   **Climb the stile at the bottom of the field, and bear right along the lane.**

Escape Route: Bear left along the lane. Avoid the gravel track on the left, then bear left at the crossroads. Follow the lane past Windgather Rocks to the starting point.

9.   **After a short way take the stile on the left, and follow the well-worn path leading downhill.**

☺ Here many young trees have been planted. Can you tell which are conifers and which are broad-leaved trees? In the middle of the field there is a small stream. In the bottom of the valley it joins another stream, Todd Brook. Together they empty into Toddbrook Reservoir, which was made by building a dam, or large wall, across the valley, so the valley became flooded. It is a few miles away at Whaley Bridge.

10. **Climb the stile and continue ahead, downhill.**

☺ In this field there are many gorse and hawthorn bushes. Gorse is very prickly with yellow flowers through most of the year. It makes a useful shelter for rabbits and hares when people are coming. Hawthorn has white or pink blossom in the Spring, and dark red berries in the Autumn. It has sharp, woody thorns.

11. **Go through the metal gate and continue downhill to the stile at the bottom.**

12. **Cross the stream and follow the path as it winds uphill. Pass the farm buildings on your left, and climb the stone stile. Continue ahead towards the house.**

Q: This is "Benthall Farm". How many chimneys does it have?

A: Three.

13. **Take the stile on the left, before the farm gates. Keep right, alongside the dry-stone wall.**

(It is possible to make a short detour here to the Tea Cosy cafe in Kettleshulme. Continue along the farm driveway and bear left to the main road. The cafe is just over the main road. Return the same way and continue with the route.)

14. **Take the stone stile at the end of the field, and head straight towards the house. Climb the makeshift stile to the right of the metal gate. Follow the gravel track past the houses.**

Q: The first house is named after a tree. What is it called?

A: "Ash Tree". These houses are "bungalows", which means they are on one level.

15. **Proceed to the lane and take the gravel track almost opposite.**

Escape Route: To return to the starting point, bear left along the lane. Keep straight ahead at the junction and follow the road. Just under 2 miles in all.

16. **Keep ahead along the track, between dry-stone walls.**

Q: The first building you pass is "Thorneycroft Farm". What are the stone animals on either side of the front door of the farmhouse?.

A: Horses.

☺ Just past the farm there are usually horses in the fields close to the trackway.

17. **Continue straight ahead.**

Q: The next building is called "Neighbourway Farm". How many chimney pots are on the main roof of the farmhouse?

A: Four.

☺ After the farmhouse there are trees overhanging the track, including sycamore, lime and horse chestnut. Do you recognise these? Sycamore trees have clusters of "keys" or "helicopters" in the Autumn. They are the tree's seeds and are blown away by the wind, sometimes quite far. This is to prevent new trees growing too near the old one. Limes, the green fruit, do not come from these lime trees which have pale green, heart-shaped leaves. In the Spring, horse chestnut trees have flowers, usually white, which look like candles. Conkers are the seeds of horse chestnut trees, and if you plant a conker, it should grow into a tree.

Escape Route: There is an unsigned footpath to the left, directly after a row of old stone cottages. Follow the track through a five-barred gate and keep straight ahead, leading uphill towards farm buildings. At the top, bear left along the farm driveway, then right at the crossroads. Follow the lane back to the starting point.

☺ After the old stone cottage you soon come to another farm. Near the top of the barn there is a square door which leads into the hayloft, where hay is stored. This has been used for hundreds of years, and is still in use. Hay is tall grass which is dried and stored in the loft, to protect it from the bad weather. It is used for Winter food for cows and horses. The Winters here can be very long and cold. It is quite common for there to be deep snow here, when there is none in the rest of the county. These lonely houses are sometimes snowed in for days. Imagine not being able to go to school until the snow melted.

18. **Go through the metal gate straight ahead, and continue along the left side of the field.**

☺ In the hedge on your left there are hawthorn and holly bushes. Both have bright red berries in the Autumn. You should be able to see Windgather Rocks on the left.

19. **At the end of the field there are two stiles. Take the wooden one on the left, next to the five-barred gate. Keep to the right of the field, heading slightly uphill towards farm buildings.**

☺ There may be sheep in this grassy field. There are about 1,000 million sheep in the world. In New Zealand there are twenty times more sheep than people!

20. **Climb the stile at the top of the field and keep straight ahead, passing the old farm buildings on the left. Go through a rusting metal gate, and take the stone stile in the dry-stone wall on the right.**

21. **Cut across the small field, keeping alongside the wooden fence on the left, and climb the stile close to the barn. Keep left, between the farm buildings, passing the farmhouse on the right, and bearing left uphill along a concrete driveway. This soon becomes a potted gravel track.**

Escape Route:Bear left and follow the drive to the crossroads. Bear right and follow the lane back to the starting point.

22. **After a short way, bear right, signed "Dunge Farm", cross the cattle grid, and follow the driveway downhill.**

☺ There are views over fields, probably with cows and sheep grazing. There are more gorse bushes, with their prickles and yellow flowers, along the driveway. Soon the drive crosses a stream. There are many trees growing close to the water, including colourful rowans, as there is some shelter from the wind, and a good supply of water.

23. **The drive becomes wide and flat on the approach to the farm. Keep straight ahead, passing the farmhouse on the left, and continue through an area of trees and shrubs, following the grassy path, signed intermittently.**

(Dunge Farm Gardens are open to the public throughout the summer. There is a "No Dogs" sign at the farm gates. This refers to visitors to the gardens, not users of the public footpath. Keep to the public right of way when passing through the gardens and keep your dog on a lead.)

Q: You should pass the farmhouse on the left. What is the date on the plaque on the front?

A: 1749

The path now passes the gardens of Dunge Farm, where there are many colourful plants and trees, growing well in this sheltered spot. Look for roses and wild dog roses.

24. **Keep ahead on the main path and cross the stream by the plank bridge.**

☺ Along the stream there are large stones and logs, covered with moss and other small, moisture-loving plants. The logs, although dead, provide a home for insects and plants. There are also blackberry bushes and ferns.

25. **Follow the path uphill to the stile. Keep left to a further stile. Keep straight ahead. At first there is a fence on the right.**

☺ Parts of this field are covered with marsh; a water-logged area. The tall, green grass with very pointed ends is marram grass. It can often be seen where it is wet, or at the seaside, in sandhills.

26. **Keep straight ahead. Soon a barn should come into view. Head for this. Pass**

the barn and cross the makeshift stile in the fence. **Follow the path ahead, keeping the fence on your left.**

Q: After a short way a rooftop should come into view straight ahead. How many chimneys does it have?

A: Two, one at each end of the main roof. This is called "Green Stack". It is a remote house, very likely to be snowed in after a heavy snowfall.

27. Keep left, now following a dry-stone wall. Follow the path downhill to a stile on the left of the house. Continue downhill and join the driveway. Almost in front of the main house, bear left and cross the stream. (There is a crossing place, but it is difficult to find in the marram grass, and the stream is narrow enough to stride across.) Head uphill, with your back to the house. There should be a clear pathway leading straight to a ladder stile over a dry-stone wall. Continue ahead to join the lane.

EscapeRoute/EndofSouthernRoute: Bear left along the lane which leads uphill. At the top bear left to the car park/starting point.

28. Bear right along the lane for a very short way.

29. Take the footpath on the left, along a farm driveway, leading downhill.

☺ The drive leads downhill, and goes over a small stream. There are many trees and prickly thistles around the water. Thistles, the emblem of Scotland, can grow quite tall and have purple flowers in the Summer. They appear on some pound coins.

You should soon see the farmhouse ahead, along the driveway. It is made of stone, and has two X's on the front. These are the ends of supports which prevent the walls from collapsing. You can often see them on old buildings.

30. Go through the wooden gate on the left, directly before the farmhouse. Climb the ladder stile on the right, labelled "Shining Tor" and "Cat & Fiddle".

Q: There should be hens in the garden of the farmhouse. Hens are female. Do you know what the male is called?

A: A cockerel.

31. Continue ahead, passing the farmhouse. Climb the next stile and follow the track uphill to the left.

☺ There may be occasional rabbit holes, or much smaller holes made by mice or voles. There should soon be views downhill, to the right, into the steep-sided valley.

32. Keep straight ahead at all times. The path soon begins to descend.

☺ Have you noticed there are no trees now? There is only grass, kept short by the sheep and cows. There is also marram grass which grows along the many small streams that run into the valley.

You may see small mounds of soil made by moles. Moles are small and mouse-like, except that they have big paws which they to dig their holes. They live underground and are very shortsighted.

33. **Climb the stile and continue ahead to a further stile, crossing several small streams.**

☺ There are no houses or trees in sight. This could seem a very lonely place if you were by yourself, but some people like this kind of solitude, away from the town and pollution.

Can you see bootprints, or the prints left by animals, in the mud on the ground?. Can you guess which print belongs to which animal? Cows have two "toes", while horses' hoofprints should show the shape of their horseshoes.
Soon you should come to a ruined house. You can see the old gateposts and the crumbling stone walls. Do not go too close, as the walls are unsafe. Never climb on old walls like these, as they are likely to collapse.

34. **Climb the stile just past the ruin, bear right and cross the stream. Follow the path uphill and bear left, passing an old stone gatepost. The stream should be just visible below, on the left, but the path soon moves away as it continues to ascend.**

35. **When the path splits, keep right, continuing uphill. It soon crosses a broken wall, and, shortly after, goes through another. The path is easier to follow from now on. There should be a fence and partially broken wall on your right. Continue uphill with the wall.**

☺ On your left there should be a steep valley with a small stream. This is the beginning of Todd Brook, which you saw earlier. It collects the rainwater that drains from the surrounding hills, and takes it to the Toddbrook Reservoir.

36. **Climb the stile and continue ahead. At the top avoid the various stiles and bear left, with the wall and fence on your right.**

☺ On the right, in the distance, you should be able to see the unmistakable outline of Shutlingsloe, a hill, which, from here, is triangular, or pyramid shaped. Below there is a road, the first sign of civilisation for some time.

37. **Follow the path as it begins the final climb. At the top, climb the stile and bear right, signed for "The Cat and Fiddle". After a very short way there is another stile on the right, which will take you to the trig. point, at the top of Shining Tor.**

☺ **(AT THE TRIG POINT)** This is Shining Tor which is on the border between the counties of Cheshire and Derbyshire. The white stone monument shows that it is the highest point in the area. Below there are fields and farms, and views in the distance towards the Cheshire Plain.

38. From the trig. Point, return over the stile and bear left. Follow the fence and wall all the way, straight ahead.

☺ It is fairly flat on the top, and often muddy, as you have probably found out! The black mud is peat, a type of soil. At one time it was cut into strips and burned on fires. This happens less often now, as peat-cutting was damaging the countryside.

The only plants growing in the peat are heather and bilberries. Both grow close to the ground and can survive the cold, wet weather and strong winds. Heather has tiny flowers of white, pink, purple or red. It is often used in gardens because it keeps its colours all year. Bilberries have light green, oval leaves, and purple-black berries in the Autumn. The fruit is sometimes used for making jam or wine.

On the right there are views into Derbyshire and towards the Goyt Valley. The moorland along the path is a "Conservation Area", which means it is a place where plants can grow without being damaged, and where animals can live safely. Do not stray from the path, as there may be birds nesting on the ground, which you would disturb and frighten.

Eventually there is a slight climb and you should be able to see rocky crags ahead, on the left. Soon there should be views down to the Goyt Forest, on the right, unless it's very misty. After a short distance it is all downhill, and not far from the end of the walk.

39. Climb the stile and descend to the road. Bear left, and then right to the car park. There are verges and paths alongside the edge of the road.

Windgather Rocks checklist

☐ HEATHER

☐ A ROCK CLIMBER

☐ AN EVERGREEN TREE

☐ A SHEEP

☐ A WHITE HOUSE

☐ A HORSE

☐ A FIRCONE

☐ A COW

☐ A STONE RUIN

☐ A CONKER/HORSE CHESTNUT TREE

💆ames for 💰oring 💆ourneys

50 Questions & Answers

Some are easy, some much more difficult. Most are mentioned in the text of the book. The answers are at the end of the section.

Cheshire

1. What is the capital city of the county of Cheshire?
2. Lewis Carroll, who wrote *"Alice in Wonderland"*, lived at Daresbury in Cheshire. Which animal character in his stories had a connection with Cheshire?
3. Chester was at one time a fort, but who built it?
   A: The Greeks   B: The Romans   C: The Chinese
4. Where in Cheshire can you see a working mill that makes cotton, and a giant waterwheel?
5. There was much fighting in Cheshire during the Civil War. Who did the government oppose in the war?
6. The Cheshire children's writer, Alan Garner, has set most of his books in the county. Do you know where his most popular book, *"The Weirdstone of Brisinghamen"* is set?
7. Do you know which large Cheshire hall has been used in many television programmes, including *"Red Dwarf"* and *"Neighbours"*?
8. Which two types of deer are found in Cheshire parkland?
9. In which Cheshire village may you find a stone elephant?
10. Whose face is carved over the well at Alderley Edge?
11. Bread is made from which crop that is grown in many places in Cheshire?
12. Do you know what "dialect" is?

See if you can guess what the following local Cheshire words mean:

13. **FLECK** – does it mean:
    A: A flea   B: A small stream   C: A female horse
14. **AGGED** – does it mean:
    A: Angry   B: Shy   C: Tired
15. **COBNOBBLE** – does it mean:
    A: To tell off   B: To win at a game   C: A type of biscuit
16. **SKEW-WIF or SKEW-WIFTER** – does it mean:
    A: A type of hat   B: Bent, or not straight   C: A type of stew
17. **ADLE** – does it mean:
    A: Lazy   B: To earn money   C: To argue

A few more Cheshire facts:

18. In which Cheshire castle have episodes of "Doctor Who" and "Sherlock Holmes" been filmed?

19. The names of several Cheshire towns end in "wich". This means they are salt mining towns. Can you name any?

20. What space-age piece of equipment would you expect to see at Jodrell Bank?

Nature

21. What is the fruit of the oak tree called?

22. Which birds are known for stealing shiny objects?

23. From which tree do conkers come?

24. Which prickly plant with red berries is often used in decorations at Christmas?

25. What is a Red Admiral?

26. What type of animal is a Red Setter?

27. What is a baby duck called?

28. That was easy, but do you know what a baby swan is called?

29. What is a rabbit's home called?

30. Some birds "migrate" in winter. What does this mean?

31. What is a deciduous tree?

32. How does a horse "groom" itself?

33. How many "toes" does a cow have?

34. Some animals, such as hedgehogs, "hibernate" in the winter. What does that mean?

35. Which small bird is famous for its red chest?

General Knowledge

36. Can you name the four points of the compass?

37. Which way does the needle on a compass always point?

38. What is the name of the Queen's famous London home?

39. Which children's programme has a colour and a boy's name in the title?

40. Do you know what glass is made from? (You find it near to the sea.)

41. What colour is produced by mixing yellow and blue paint?

42. In Britain, do cars drive on the right or the left of the road?

43. What is the name for a book which gives the meaning of words?

44. In which country do the men traditionally wear kilts?

45. How many sides are there to a rectangle?

46. What is the name of the Queen's eldest son?

47. Do you know what the capital of France is?

48. How many pennies are there in a pound?
49. How many 5 pences are there in a pound?
50. How many numbers are there on a telephone?

Answers

1. Chester.
2. The Cheshire Cat.
3. B – The Romans.
4. Quarry Bank Mill, Styal.
5. The King, Charles I.
6. Alderley Edge.
7. Lyme Hall.
8. Red and Fallow Deer are the most common.
9. Peckforton.
10. The Wizard of Alderley.
11. Wheat, though bread can be made of other grains as well.
12. It is a local way of speaking.
13. A – A flea.
14. C – Tired.
15. A – To tell off.
16. B – Bent, not straight.
17. B – To earn money.
18. Peckforton Castle.
19. Northwich, Middlewich & Nantwich.
20. The huge white dish of the radio telescope.
21. An Acorn.
22. Magpies.
23. Horse Chestnut.
24. Holly.
25. A Butterfly.
26. A Dog.
27. A Duckling.
28. A Cygnet.
29. A Burrow or Warren.
30. They fly south to warmer countries.
31. It loses its leaves in winter.
32. By rolling over.
33. Two, or rather each hoof is split in two.

34. They go to sleep until the spring.
35. A Robin, or Robin Red Breast.
36. North, south, east and west.
37. North.
38. Buckingham Palace.
39. Blue Peter.
40. Sand.
41. Green.
42. Left.
43. A dictionary.
44. Scotland.
45. Four.
46. Prince Charles.
47. Paris.
48. One hundred.
49. Twenty.
50. Ten.

Ideas for Games on Long Journeys

1. If you are in a car, you will pass many roadsigns. Children can have about eight secondsworth of fun guessing what each sign means, and may also retain some helpful knowledge for later in life.
2. Think of a subject e.g. animals, birds, trees, and each child or member of the party has to say a type of animal. After a few rounds, it will get more difficult. If you can't answer you are out. The winner, obviously, is the one remaining at the end.
3. I-Spy, an old favourite.
4. Guess who? Think of a famous person, cartoon character etc. and the children have to guess who it is by asking questions (to which you give yes/no answers) such as: Are you a woman? Are you on television? Give them the odd clue occasionally to help them along.
5. Counting things. On a car journey, the most obvious subject would be cars. Each person picks a different coloured car, the winner is the one who has pointed out the most at the end of the journey.